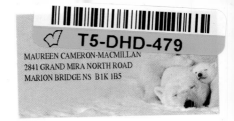

ᓀᐱᖏᑦ ᑕᑌᐅᔅᔦᔐᐊᒥᐅᑦ

La Baie : cœur et âme

ᑎᒥᖅ ᐴᕐ ᐊᐅᑎᐅᑕᑯᔨᐧᑖ ᐃᔭᔕᐧᐊᐃᖕ

Voices from the Bay

**Traditional Ecological Knowledge
of Inuit and Cree
in the Hudson Bay Bioregion**

Voices from the Bay

Compiled by
**Miriam McDonald
Lucassie Arragutainaq
Zack Novalinga**

**Canadian Arctic Resources Committee
Environmental Committee of Municipality of Sanikiluaq**

Canadian Cataloguing in Publication Data

McDonald, Miriam Anne, 1959-
Voices from the bay: traditional ecological
knowledge of Inuit and Cree in the Hudson Bay
bioregion

ISBN 0-919996-75-2

1. Environmental impact analysis–Hudson Bay
Region. 2. Ecology–Hudson Bay Region. 3. Cree
Indians–Hudson Bay Region. 4. Inuit–Hudson Bay
Region. I. Arragutainaq, Lucassie, 1950- II. Novalinga,
Zacharassie, 1947- III. Canadian Arctic Resources
Committee IV. Environmental Committee of
Sanikiluaq V. Title.

GF512.H83M33 1997   C96-900846-5
              333.7'14'089970714111

Canadian Arctic Resources Committee
One Nicholas Street, Suite 1100
Ottawa, Ontario K1N 7B7

Municipality of Sanikiluaq
Sanikiluaq, N.W.T. X0A 0W0

Please note: Orders for *Voices from the Bay* will be filled from the CARC Ottawa office only.

For generations, Cree and Inuit Elders have passed on their knowledge of animals and the environment to their sons and daughters to enable them to support their families.

This book is dedicated to those teachings and to the Elders, hunters, and trappers who have come forward during the Hudson Bay Programme to record and share their traditional ecological knowledge.

The world can tell us everything we want to know. The only problem for the world is that it doesn't have a voice. But the world's indicators are there. They are always talking to us.

Quitsak Tarkiasuk

Contents

List of Figures

Acknowledgements

Many people and institutions with little history of working together—federal, provincial, and territorial governments, electric utility companies, private consultants, aboriginal peoples' organizations, public-interest organizations, and the residents of the region, particularly Inuit and Cree—collaborated to make possible the Hudson Bay Traditional Ecological Knowledge and Management Systems (TEKMS) study. We thank all involved, especially the Inuit and Cree, who provided the information found in this book. The dedication and language skills of the translators deserve special recognition; without them, this valuable source of knowledge would not be documented in English.

Members of the Elders Committee and the Technical Advisory Committee provided constructive input and advice throughout the study. We learned, and hope to continue learning, from Fred Beardy, Nala Nappaaluk, Fikret Berkes, Milton Freeman, Robbie Keith, Bob Milko, Peter Sly, and Buster Welch.

We thank all who organized the meetings and helped compile and synthesize the information: Naomi Akavak, Michael Anderson, Charlie Arngak, Helen Atkinson, Louis Bird, Helen Fast, Nicole Gombay, Alison Haugh, Stewart Hill, Nellie Ippak, Titi Kadluk, Sarah Kalff, Peter Kattuk, Jeannie Kittosuk, John Ningeongan, Kate Romanow, Donald Saunders, Talbot Saunders, John Turner, John Sallenave, and Paul Sammurtok. A special thanks to Ray Edamura for setting up a computer system that enabled us to "take the walrus by the tusks," to Michael Francis and Edie Van Alstine for editing, and to Anne Kneif for production and layout.

The original partners—Rawson Academy of Aquatic Science, Canadian Arctic Resources Committee, and the Environmental Committee of Sanikiluaq—deserve special acknowledgement for designing and promoting the Hudson Bay Programme and the Traditional Ecological Knowledge and Management Systems study. Thanks are also due to Glen Okrainetz, initial manager of the Hudson Bay Programme, and to Terry Fenge, whose perseverance has made possible the publication of *Voices from the Bay*.

The TEKMS study of the Hudson Bay Programme was made possible by the financial support of foundations in Canada and the United States, agencies of the Canadian and Northwest Territories governments, industry, and regional aboriginal organizations. This collaboration was most welcome; we hope it can be repeated in other studies. Funding agencies are sometimes wary of innovative projects such as the traditional ecological research reported in this book, but those listed below realized the importance of the work we intended. Quite simply, the financial support of these agencies made our work possible:

Richard and Jean Ivey Fund
Harold Crabtree Foundation
Walter and Duncan Gordon Charitable Foundation
McLean Foundation
George Cedric Metcalf Charitable Foundation
Helen McCrea Peacock Foundation
Murphy Foundation Incorporated
John D. and Catherine T. MacArthur Foundation
Molson Family Foundation
EJLB Foundation
Government of the Northwest Territories
Indian and Northern Affairs Canada
Department of Fisheries and Oceans
Environment Canada
Ontario Hydro
Hydro-Québec
Grand Council of the Crees (of Québec)
Mushkegowuk Tribal Council
Nunavut Wildlife Management Board
Nunavut Tunngavik Incorporated

"We, as aboriginal people, are part of the land and water. We recognize and respect the delicate balance of nature for the total existence of all living things including those we see physically, and those we don't.... Once these natural processes are disturbed and denied their natural flow, the aboriginal people of this country are adversely affected. Taking away the land and water takes away our pride, dignity, and ability to survive."

Foreword

It has been nearly thirty years since environmental concerns first gained the attention of politicians, yet we continue to struggle with the most basic questions: How and for what purpose shall we develop our natural resources? What are the human and environmental implications of our decisions?

In ecologically vulnerable northern Canada these questions are particularly important. This vast region is home to aboriginal peoples with their own ideas about what should happen in their traditional territories. In the last twenty-five years, Inuit, Dene, Cree, and Métis have had some success articulating, defining, and defending their rights and interests; nevertheless, industrialism continues to move north with potentially serious environmental and social effects.

Although the Canadian North remains physically remote from the south and from the broader world, pollutants inevitably find their way there. Scientists now characterize the Arctic as a "sink," the final resting place for many contaminants used in industry and agriculture thousands of kilometres away. These contaminants—particularly organochlorines—are persistent, entering the food chain and bioaccumulating in each level. Inuit and other aboriginal peoples are exposed to health risks as they ingest such contaminants when eating traditional food.

Base and precious metal mines with their required infrastructure—roads, airstrips, and ports—are now a permanent feature of the north. Diamond mining is under way north of Yellowknife. Oil and gas exploration continues in the Mackenzie valley and delta. And many rivers in the northern portions of Quebec, Ontario, and Manitoba have been dammed for their hydroelectric potential.

In the late 1980s and early 1990s the developmental spotlight in the north was focused on Hydro-Québec's plans to develop the hydroelectric potential of the Great Whale River. The La Grande River system had already been developed, and harnessing the Nottaway-Broadback system was proposed for early in the twenty-first century. Significant hydro power development was in place in northern Ontario and northern Manitoba, and additional projects were on the drawing boards. Just what the combined and cumulative effects of these and further projects on the Hudson Bay bioregion might be, and whether existing or proposed developments breached sustainable limits, was anyone's guess. Governments were ill-disposed to find out and each guarded its political and administrative jurisdictions jealously.

Aboriginal peoples expect resource development in their homelands to be assessed for ecological sustainability and to provide sustainable social, cultural, and economic benefits. Although ecological sustainability is a concept that wins almost unanimous support, it remains difficult to translate into decisions and action and is especially elusive in the north, where scientific information is sparse. This is where aboriginal peoples' traditional ecological knowledge (TEK) can make an important contribution.

TEK was a very significant component of the Hudson Bay Programme—a research and advocacy programme on existing and potential impacts in Hudson Bay of development occurring within its watershed. This book—*Voices from the Bay*—reports what Inuit and Cree in Hudson and James bay communities said about the changes occurring in their natural environment.

To southerners, the sheer size of Hudson Bay and its surrounding watershed is beguiling; human activity appears small, even insignificant, within this whole. But such is not the perception of the Inuit and Cree who live there and must adjust to both human-induced and natural changes to the environment. Aboriginal cultures and economies are under great stress as "modernity" reaches into their homelands; so too is the natural environment upon which the Inuit and Cree so heavily rely.

This book is the first—and not the last—word about TEK and environmental change in the Hudson Bay bioregion as a whole. The research was designed and conducted by aboriginal people, and its geographical scope is immense. Please listen to these voices from the bay.

Terry Fenge
Former Executive Director
Canadian Arctic Resources Committee

December 1996

"Cree and Inuit may have different cultures but one thing we think alike on is preservation of the animals and environment. We preserve the environment because it is the place where we hunt the animals for food. If we're going to live a good life, our environment has to be clean."

Introduction

We, native people, have lived in our land since time immemorial. We know our lands, are experts in our environment. We do not study it for just a few years. It is a lifetime study. It is knowledge from the beginning passed on to us by our Ancestors. We have knowledge, true knowledge because it's our way of life.

Titi Kadluk, Chesterfield Inlet

We are the last human beings on this planet who can give this information to the white governments of this great land of ours that we call Canada.

Robbie Matthews, Chisasibi

Hudson Bay, including James Bay, Hudson Strait, and all interconnecting channels, is one of the world's largest inland seas. It is bounded by Quebec, Ontario, Manitoba, and the Northwest Territories, but falls under federal jurisdiction. Provinces and the Northwest Territories, however, exert significant influence over the bay through the industrial activities and land and resource uses they allow in the upstream watershed.

The expansion of development throughout the Hudson Bay bioregion—particularly over the last 50 years—has raised ecological, social, cultural, and economic concerns, especially among aboriginal peoples who live in the region.[1] Large-scale hydroelectric projects, mining activity, logging, and community development are most obviously contributing to changes in the natural environment.

Naturally occurring environmental change also affects the cultures and economies of the aboriginal peoples—Inuit and Cree—living in this bioregion (figure 1). Not surprisingly, scientists have only a partial understanding of the scale, pace, and causes of environmental change in Hudson Bay, for relatively little scientific research has been carried out. Moreover, the social and other consequences of this change—natural and human-induced—have yet to be fully addressed.

The Inuit and Cree of the Hudson Bay bioregion have a unique sense of environmental change in this region. They have accumulated and passed on, for many generations, a collective body of knowledge based on observation of the environment and experience while hunting, fishing, trapping, and gathering. This oral tradition goes beyond simply documenting events: it represents an understanding of complex relationships in the natural environment that influence the behaviour of animals and indigenous peoples.

The traditional ecological knowledge (TEK) of aboriginal peoples has rarely been considered by government agencies, industry, scientists, or others and has even been dismissed by some officials as anecdotal or culturally determined. Nevertheless, in recent years there has been a growing consensus among academics and others that TEK needs to be considered; for example, TEK is incorporated into the guidelines for environmental and social impact assessment of the proposed Great Whale hydroelectric development in northern Quebec.

In the aftermath of the 1992 Earth Summit in Brazil, the federal and most provincial governments in Canada have embraced "sustainability" as a core concept to guide future resource development. Sustainability requires that economic development be conducted in the most environmentally benign manner possible, recognizing inherent "limits" in the earth's capacity to provide resources for human use and to assimilate resulting wastes. Many Cree and Inuit question whether existing and planned resource developments in their homelands will breach or have already breached sustainable limits in the Hudson Bay bioregion. They suggest that TEK might be used in a cumulative impact assessment (CIA) to find answers and that TEK could assist in implementing the principle of sustainability. Their questions, and the sense that TEK might assist in making environmentally and socially responsible decisions for the bioregion, prompted the Environmental Committee of Sanikiluaq to conduct a three-year study into the views and traditional ecological knowledge of Cree and Inuit living in the region (figure 2).

The emphasis of the work was on some of the ecological relationships and changes in those relationships that the indigenous peoples of Hudson Bay have observed over time, and particularly over the past 50 years.

1

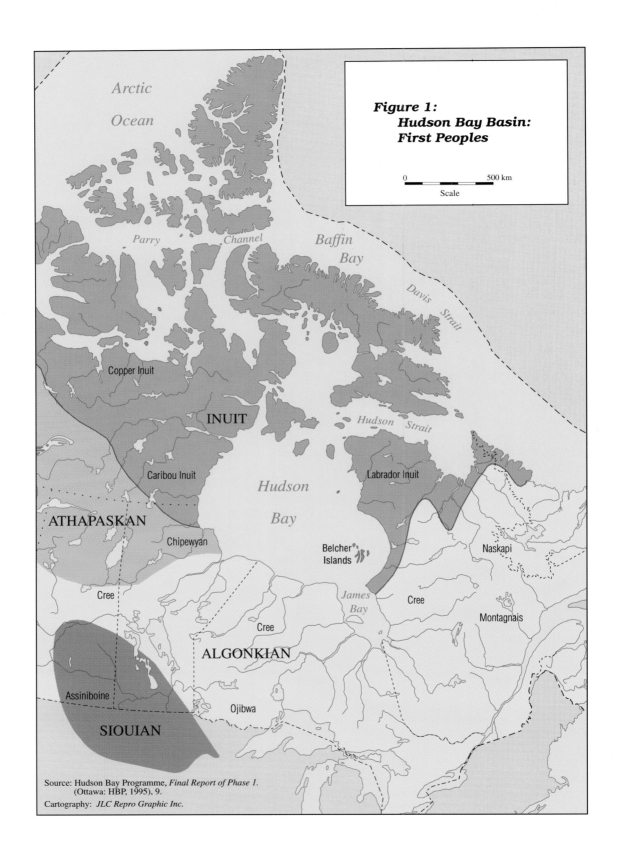

Figure 1:
Hudson Bay Basin:
First Peoples

0   500 km
Scale

Arctic

Ocean

Parry   Channel   Baffin
                            Bay

                            Davis
                            Strait

Copper Inuit

INUIT   Hudson   Strait

Caribou Inuit   Labrador Inuit

ATHAPASKAN   Hudson

Chipewyan   Bay

                            Belcher   Naskapi
                            Islands

Cree   James
                            Bay
            Cree   Cree
                                            Montagnais
        ALGONKIAN

Assiniboine
            Ojibwa

SIOUIAN

Source: Hudson Bay Programme, *Final Report of Phase 1.*
    (Ottawa: HBP, 1995), 9.
Cartography: *JLC Repro Graphic Inc.*

Figure 2: Hudson Bay TEKMS Study Area

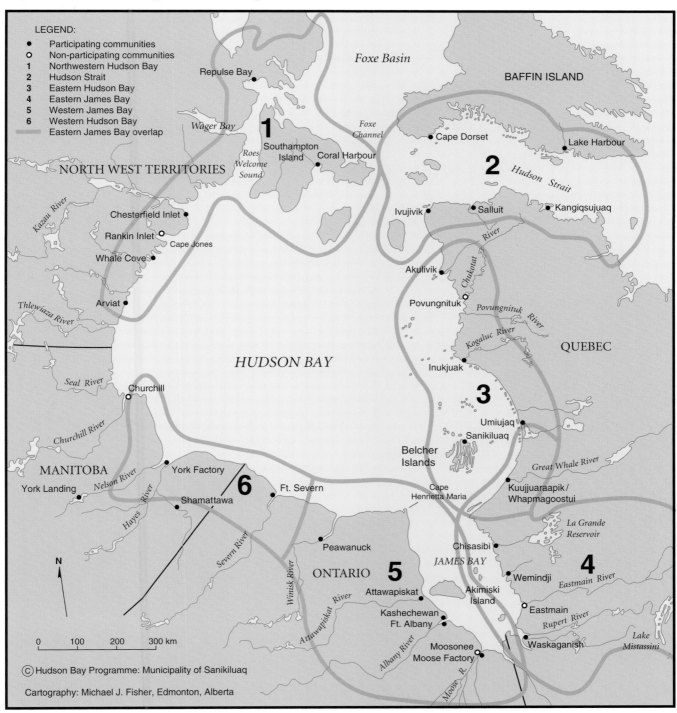

LEGEND:
- ● Participating communities
- ○ Non-participating communities
- **1** Northwestern Hudson Bay
- **2** Hudson Strait
- **3** Eastern Hudson Bay
- **4** Eastern James Bay
- **5** Western James Bay
- **6** Western Hudson Bay
- ─── Eastern James Bay overlap

Foxe Basin

BAFFIN ISLAND

Repulse Bay

Foxe Channel

Wager Bay

1

Cape Dorset

Lake Harbour

Roes Welcome Sound

Southampton Island

Coral Harbour

NORTH WEST TERRITORIES

2

Hudson Strait

Kazan River

Ivujivik

Salluit

Kangiqsujuaq

Chesterfield Inlet

Rankin Inlet

Cape Jones

Whale Cove

Akulivik

Chukotat River

Thlewiaza River

Arviat

Povungnituk

Povungnituk River

Kogaluc River

QUEBEC

Inukjuak

HUDSON BAY

3

Seal River

Churchill

Umiujaq

Sanikiluaq

Belcher Islands

Great Whale River

Churchill River

MANITOBA

York Factory

York Landing

Nelson River

6

Ft. Severn

Cape Henrietta Maria

Kuujjuaraapik/ Whapmagoostui

La Grande Reservoir

Hayes River

Shamattawa

Severn River

Peawanuck

Chisasibi

JAMES BAY

N

Winisk River

ONTARIO

5

Attawapiskat

Akimiski Island

Wemindji

Eastmain River

4

Attawapiskat River

Kashechewan

Ft. Albany

Eastmain

Rupert River

Lake Mistassini

0 100 200 300 km

Albany River

Moosonee Moose Factory

Waskaganish

Moose R.

© Hudson Bay Programme: Municipality of Sanikiluaq

Cartography: Michael J. Fisher, Edmonton, Alberta

Source: Hudson Bay Programme, *Traditional Ecological Knowledge of Environmental Changes in Hudson and James Bays, Part I.* (Ottawa: HBP, 1995), 4.

In this programme, we are attempting to tap into traditional knowledge from around Hudson and James bays because we will need some reference that we can look back on. We will need records ... because if there is to be mining, oil exploration, or hydroelectric dams, we know that they will affect our wildlife, ice, and marine areas. We have knowledge in those areas. Our knowledge is in our heads: our fathers' and grandfathers' knowledge is in our heads. We are trying to put that knowledge to use ... because we can get a much better and bigger picture of the area when we have people from all areas of Hudson and James bays participating.

Peter Kattuk, Sanikiluaq

In undertaking this research programme, Inuit and Cree suggested that the federal government and appropriate provincial and territorial governments co-operatively undertake a CIA of development in the Hudson Bay bioregion. This has yet to take place. Nevertheless, the need for a CIA was recognized in the early 1990s, when public policy makers, scientists, and aboriginal peoples raised important questions about the nature and human ecological effects of large-scale industrial development. Most development had proceeded project by project without assessment of the system-wide changes or effects. Many river diversions and damming schemes, for example, already existed when utilities in Ontario, Quebec, and Manitoba announced plans in the late 1980s to construct additional hydroelectric complexes. These and other proposed developments led to three basic questions central to sustainability and CIA: What changes are occurring in the natural environment as a result of increased human activity in Hudson Bay? How are the impacts of large-scale resource extraction industries affecting the natural order? What are the long-term implications for the people and fauna of the region who depend upon the natural resources for their food and livelihood?

Research process

The research reported in this book was initiated in 1992 and completed in 1995. From the outset, the Traditional Ecological Knowledge and Management Systems (TEKMS) study was community based and community controlled. The mayor of Sanikiluaq invited 30 communities to participate, and during the following two-and-a-half years 78 individuals—Elders or active hunters from 28 communities—did so. The research was co-ordinated from Sanikiluaq.

The research process included two study workshops in October 1992 and January 1994, 12 regional workshops in communities around the bay, and, in April 1994, a workshop convening scientists and community representatives. As well, the research team met with the Elders Committee and the Technical Advisory Committee on several occasions.

From the communities' perspective, the goals of the workshops were as follows:

- to share information;
- to understand better the environmental changes caused by development;
- to identify cumulative environmental impacts of development;
- to gather baseline information to measure future impacts;
- to help scientists understand environmental change and problems; and
- to promote the use of traditional knowledge to conserve and manage the environment.

The first series of regional workshops—comprising six four-day sessions—gathered, shared, recorded, and mapped TEK. Each followed the same discussion agenda—study purpose, weather, rivers, shorelines, currents, ice, animals, traditional management, human health, and effects of development—and was conducted in either Cree or Inuttitut with English translation. All statements were recorded on audio cassette and translated and transcribed into English for analysis. Participants at each workshop spent at least one day recording TEK on map overlays. Geographical Information System (GIS) principles were applied during data gathering to integrate map overlays and text.

The second series of regional workshops, to verify information, began once proceedings from the first series had been compiled and organized by the study team. Workshop participants spent three days clarifying information from maps, charts, and transcripts based on common themes and specific questions for each area.

4

Further information about the research methods used to gather and, in particular, to synthesize traditional ecological knowledge is included in appendix A.

Environmental views and values

From the perspective of TEK, the identification of changes for cumulative impact assessment cannot be restricted to those changes occurring in the biophysical realm. Both Cree and Inuit consider themselves integral components of the Hudson Bay ecosystem and, at the end of the 20th century, wish to maintain traditional relations with the natural environment. Thus it is important to consider some of their values to appreciate how they view, understand, and relate to the natural environment.

The importance of respect

The word respect is key to understanding wildlife and environment. If there is no respect then environmental problems arise. Everything in the environment has a place and use by people and wildlife. So, damage to any of these causes problems. We learn something about currents, ice, river systems, snow cover, and animals every day and all these things have to be respected. Respect towards nature is needed in order to have food and a good living.

Lucassie Arragutainaq, Sanikiluaq

We have been told from our Ancestors that all the animals have to be treated properly. Even small animals that live on this planet serve a purpose. Flies, for instance, are annoying but their purpose is to clean up. The shrimp eat decaying matter, and serve as cleaning agents in the sea.

Eli Kimaliardjuk, Chesterfield Inlet; Jack Angoo, Whale Cove

When something in the environment changes you follow the change and look at the area where the change is occurring because when one thing changes everything around it also changes and we, as people, have to change along with it. Respect for the environment, therefore, is very important because it guides us in how we treat the environment. We know that lack of respect can cause a lot of changes.

Lucassie Arragutainaq, Sanikiluaq

During workshop 2, Inuit and Cree agreed that they share the same values in handling and respecting animals *according to nature's way*. They believe humans should not interfere with animals' *ways of being*. Animals should be *free to live* and are given to Inuit and Cree, when needed, with the Creator's help. As children, traditional Inuit and Cree were taught—and they teach their children—not to hurt wildlife.

The natural environment

We, as aboriginal people, are part of the land and water.... we recognize and respect the delicate balance of nature for the total existence of all living things including those we see physically, and those we don't. The Creator gave us that understanding and knowledge to visualize the harmonious relationships we have with our lands and water.... Our Elders and Ancestors taught us ways to survive in co-existence with our environment. The Elders taught people how to provide medicine from the natural healing processes of nature. Once these natural processes are disturbed and denied their natural flow, the aboriginal people of this country are adversely affected.... Taking away the land and water takes away our pride, dignity and ability to survive.

Donald Saunders, York Landing

The Creator put Mother Nature on earth to provide for us. If there are great changes to the [Great Whale] river system something will definitely happen in the future.... With all the changes to Mother Earth, everybody is being affected: human beings, waterfowl, and animals.

John Petagumskum, Whapmagoostui

Everything created on this earth was put in its natural place. The Creator decided where everything, including all plant life, should be.... People have their place in the environment along with the animals. In the time when only Cree and Inuit were out on the land there was nothing to disturb the animals and plants. At that time, everything in the natural world spoke for itself. People were so connected with nature that they knew and read its signs.... The Elders watched and kept track of everything around them. They closely observed the animals in order to predict the weather.

John Petagumskum, Whapmagoostui

As Inuit, we have knowledge about animals vanishing for periods of time. From the Elders, we know ... all the sea water mammals including beluga whales are like that. One day there are too many of them so they vanish for a period of time and come back later on. Our Elders ... told us, "you don't give up because one day there will be nothing. The next day there will be something in the same area."

Simeonie Akpik, Lake Harbour

They knew because it happened before. They were telling us from past experience because there used to be lots of animals, then they almost disappeared and then they came back in large numbers.

Johnny Kavik, Sanikiluaq

The land was always shared with the animals, and our Ancestors understood their movements very well.... Our people knew where the caribou would winter and where they would stop. It's the same thing for migrating birds. Our people had a special place for them to eat. They understood the kind of land they needed, and that the birds would give us a food supply.... All the hunters and young hunters-to-be were told where to hunt, and where not to hunt. The birds knew where they had a priority, and where they could eat properly and be healthy. Only when the right season arrived did the people hunt them....

Louis Bird, Peawanuck

When we talk about the hunting territory, the person never just thinks of himself. He thinks also of his children and his grandchildren. He thinks about how he will leave this land and what state it will be in when his children and grandchildren get it. He lived off this land....

John Matches, Wemindji

Environmental responsibility

Inuit and Cree know we should have a clean environment in order to make our bodies, animals and the environment function well. The environment must remain healthy because people have to rely on it for food. The animals are part of our life, and have to be looked after very carefully....

Lucassie Arragutainaq, Sanikiluaq

It was Inuit law not to abuse or play with animals and, even today, I'm really afraid to break those laws. I've taught my children and grandchildren not to abuse them either. Also, we are taught not to wound an animal if we aren't going to eat it.... My father told me if I wound an animal I shouldn't make it suffer because it also hurts inside when in pain.

Matilda Sulurayok, Arviat; John Kaunak, Repulse Bay

Since time immemorial, the natives were put here ... to take care of the land. Our grandfathers did not abuse the land and it's our turn to pass our knowledge on to our younger generation. What our forefathers kept all this time is very precious. It's now in our hands. Our Creator has given us the responsibility for taking very good care of what we have. If we don't take care of it we will lose our own culture one day.

John Petagumskum, Whapmagoostui

Inuit and Cree suggest that TEK should be used in planning, assessment, and political processes to make decisions about the future of the region. They see TEK as a web of relations between people and the land that needs to be understood if both are to be sustained. Herein lies the possibility of common ground for aboriginal peoples, agencies of government, industry, and business.

Even with the goodwill of all parties concerned, bringing sound environmental decision making to Hudson Bay will prove difficult. Fragmented jurisdiction, differing environmental and procedural standards, sometimes competing institutions, information deficiencies, financial constraints, and other factors will have to be overcome to ensure sustainable resource use in the bioregion.

Voices from the Bay documents Inuit and Cree observations of stresses to and changes in the Hudson Bay environment. These changes are expressed in terms that are easy to understand and are illustrated with observations of animals of immediate cultural and economic importance to Cree and Inuit and of environmental factors of importance to everyone. The book includes a number of "indicators" used by indigenous peoples in the region to suggest environmental changes and concludes that currents, rivers, sea ice, and the health of humans and of the animals they eat are the most vital indicators of environmental change in the region.

A word on intellectual property rights

Respect and trust are fundamental principles that underlay the development and conduct of this particular study. The Hudson Bay Programme recognized the intellectual property rights of the community participants who provided cultural knowledge that was recorded and documented in the Hudson Bay TEKMS study. The decisions of funding agencies to support the study, and of individual community representatives to communicate knowledge and information, were made on the recognition by the Hudson Bay Programme that "knowledge belongs to the people it comes from and respect is the fundamental principle of the Hudson Bay TEKMS Study. Active aboriginal harvesters and Elders are respected as primary holders of traditional ecological knowledge; and, in this study, they have the opportunity to communicate knowledge at their discretion in a language of their preference."[2]

Similarly, community decisions to participate in the study were made on the basis that "the Hudson Bay Programme realizes aboriginal people deserve an equal or greater contribution from others in the programme's sustainable development initiative and partnership. It further acknowledges that in sharing traditional ecological knowledge, indigenous peoples of Hudson and James bays are pursuing the opportunity to create a sustainable future because they want to see changes in, and be part of decisions made with regard to, the use and management of environments that sustain themselves and all other living resources within the region."[3]

To this end, the Hudson Bay Programme applied principles of community participatory research, so that

- development and implementation of the TEKMS study was guided by the aboriginal peoples, communities, and regional agencies directly involved;
- training was provided to encourage the use and application of TEKMS;

- a designated agency in each area received a complete set of its communities' raw data including cassette tapes, transcripts, and maps;
- study opportunities, progress reports, and results were communicated to participating communities; and
- a designated agency in each area received reports, publications, and map reproductions from the study.

The study is both unique and historic because for the first time traditional Cree and Inuit have come together to record cultural knowledge for the benefit of their environments and communities. There was a subtle but nevertheless poignant realization that they were not simply providers of information, but rather researchers doing their own study. A strong sense of ownership evolved from increasing awareness among the community participants of the value in their knowledge and from appreciation for the quality of information being developed into text and map databases.

As a result, Inuit and Cree participants passed a resolution concerning storage, handling, and use of original data. The chair of the Sanikiluaq Environmental Committee made a clear commitment that, although study results were meant to be used publicly, other uses of the data would be based on further discussion among the communities.

Notes

1. The terms Hudson Bay and Hudson Bay bioregion refer to marine, coastal, and riverine areas of Hudson Bay, James Bay, and Hudson Strait.
2. Hudson Bay Programme, 1992. *Proposal for Funding: Sustainable Development in the Hudson Bay–James Bay Bioregion.* Canadian Arctic Resources Committee; Environmental Committee, Municipality of Sanikiluaq; and Rawson Academy of Aquatic Science.
3. *Ibid.*

" The word respect is key to understanding wildlife and environment. If there is no respect then environmental problems arise."

Traditional Knowledge of Ecosystem Components

The world can tell us everything we want to know. The only problem for the world is that it doesn't have a voice. But the world's indicators are there. They are always talking to us.

Quitsak Tarkiasuk, Ivujivik

Hudson Bay Cree and Inuit have knowledge about many of the natural processes occurring in their ecosystem. Seasonal cycles, rivers, currents, sea ice, the food web, and seasonal foods are particularly important to Hudson Bay aboriginal peoples. Their knowledge of these elements of the ecosystem, founded on respect for the environment and its processes and for the wildlife with which they share the region's land and waters, has sustained their traditional lifestyles.

Seasonal cycles

The Hudson Bay annual seasonal cycle has two important turning points: when the warm air cools as the cycle turns towards freezing, and when the first warm air breaks the deep cold in the late months of winter.

The region starts to transform into a colder environment towards the end of August or during September. Early indicators are birds migrating south, fish migrating upriver, vegetation changing colour, leaves falling, and the occurrence of frost. In the Hudson Strait area, Inuit recognize *early fall* as snow geese arrive from the north, caribou shed their antler velvet, and Arctic char migrate upriver. Later, *fall* arrives as the beluga whales and seals migrate to winter locations and the walrus move inshore. In western Hudson Bay, *fall* coincides with young birds flying for the first time; and in eastern James Bay, with the whitefish and lake trout spawning and the caribou mating.

During this transition to fall, precipitation is usually more frequent than in summer and, as air temperatures drop, rain changes to ice-pellet showers and blowing snow. Meltwater pools and ponds are first to freeze, followed by the land, lakes, and rivers as cooler air temperatures prevail. Sea ice first forms within inlets and along shorelines. By the end of the transition, both animals and humans have adapted to Hudson Bay's winter environment.

Residents observe the spring turning point during *mid-winter* in James Bay, *towards spring* in western Hudson Bay, in *early spring* in eastern and northwestern Hudson Bay, and with the arrival of *long days* in Hudson Strait. After an initial warm spell, the atmosphere often cools again while the environment responds gradually to warmer air temperatures, longer days, and the sun rising higher in the sky. In Hudson Strait, the clouds are higher, seals bask on the ice, and ptarmigan return from the south. Eagles return to western Hudson Bay. In eastern Hudson Bay, landforms emerge from beneath snow and ice cover and Canada geese begin to arrive. In James Bay, sea and freshwater ice have attained maximum thickness before break-up.

As the cold air warms, frequent snowstorms in some areas allow snow to accumulate further. A critical factor during the spring transition occurs when melted snow refreezes, making feeding difficult for caribou, reindeer, fox, Arctic hare, and ptarmigan. Unable to penetrate the hard layer of ice to reach lemmings and mice under the frozen snow, foxes move to the sea shoreline in search of food.

[Please see appendix B for more extensive descriptions of the seasonal characteristics in different areas of the Hudson Bay region.]

Forecasting

Traditional Cree and Inuit have acquired the interpretive skills and adaptive strategies needed to respond to seasonal changes and to the different environmental conditions that influence animal behaviour. Traditionally, they predict seasonal characteristics, adjust to seasonal change, and forecast daily weather using their knowledge of clouds, stars, northern lights, wind, snow, ice, currents, and animal behaviour under different environmental conditions.

Inuit in the Hudson Strait area expect bad weather that day or the next when *caribou or seals shake their heads.* In spring, Inuit expect bad weather when

northbound geese reverse direction. They anticipate very bad weather when the geese do not move. In eastern Hudson Bay, they know poorer weather will probably come the next day when *echoes travel for miles*. Eastern James Bay residents predict a storm when a haze forms out in the bay. In Hudson Strait, birds gathering in large numbers or animals moving in the same direction is a sign of a storm building; geese flying high signals better weather.

In western Hudson Bay, part of the day will be cold when *the woodpecker's beak moves fast*, and it will be extremely cold when bright northern lights cover the entire sky. Northern lights appearing *reddish-orange on their southern side* portend warmer weather for about three days. When chickadees arrive suddenly on a cold day, milder weather is expected the next day.

Strong winds are anticipated in Hudson Strait when a dark cloud appears from nowhere and then disappears. When clouds move counter-clockwise, it is unlikely winds will decrease; when they blow clockwise, winds are expected to abate.

In eastern Hudson Bay, the appearance of dark clouds with white, round clouds just as the sun is about to set on a nice calm day suggests snow the next day. In western Hudson Bay, snow is expected when the owls call at night.

When rabbit paws turn white earlier than usual in western James Bay, Cree expect an early snowfall and a difficult winter. The occurrence of small offspring from beaver or moose suggests a long winter. In western Hudson Bay, thunder in late fall is a sign of a warmer-than-usual winter and thunder early in spring means a hot summer.

Sea mammals return to the Cape Dorset area soon after the eider ducks, and in western Hudson Bay an abnormal influx of wolves signals high caribou numbers. A sudden population explosion of mice during summer can mean a high fox population in western Hudson Bay. When snow birds arrive first from the east, geese will be plentiful; when first from the west, geese will not be plentiful. In western James Bay two stars on the north and south sides of the moon suggest moose nearby.

[Please see appendix C for an extensive listing of environmental indicators traditionally used by Cree and Inuit in the bioregion.]

Currents

Currents give life to everything that lives in oceans. If there were no currents, the water would be like lake water and the marine mammals and birds would disappear.

Lucassie Iqaluk, Inukjuak

The currents clean everything, and lots of our animals depend on the currents for survival. If there were no currents the ice would get very thick, even in deeper water. The water never stops moving, so it helps the animals and humans alike. If the water stopped moving, the animals in the marine world would stop moving, and Inuit would have nothing to eat.

Lucassie Iqaluk, Inukjuak

Hudson Bay surface water generally circulates in a counter-clockwise direction (figure 3). The circulation is driven by tidal flow and often this is strengthened by the additional influence of wind and river discharge. A forceful current in Roes Welcome Sound moves water southward past the western Hudson Bay communities of Rankin Inlet, Whale Cove, and Arviat to Churchill. Inshore currents move the water southeasterly from Churchill to Cape Henrietta Maria.

Strong currents by Cape Henrietta Maria circulate Hudson Bay water into James Bay, where it continues south to the mouth of the Attawapiskat River. The current splits in the channel between the Attawapiskat River and Akimiski Island. On one side of the island the water turns north; on the other it flows south towards Moosonee, where currents circulate water northward between islands and along the east coast of James Bay up into eastern Hudson Bay. A strong offshore current moves the water northward and eastward through Hudson Strait.

Traditional Cree and Inuit recognize the more than 500 rivers flowing into Hudson and James bays as important generators of marine currents:

The rivers really boost the marine current system because so many of them flow into Hudson Bay. The freshwater pushes the sea water, and the volume of water coming in from the rivers makes the currents stronger. I think the marine currents would be much slower inside Hudson Bay if the rivers were not flowing into it.

Lucassie Iqaluk, Inukjuak; Joshua Sala, Umiujaq

At the floe edge, in winter, we see the current is stronger when situated near a river. Those of us who have been near the rivers know that.

Peter Alogut, Coral Harbour

Inuit in northwestern Hudson Bay say *strength of the current differs annually because each year is different.* Cape Dorset Inuit observe strong currents every four or five years, whereas Inukjuak Inuit report that open water beyond the floe edge that used to freeze over every seven or eight years has been freezing annually in recent years.

The distance from land to the floe edge varies with current force and temperature and, some years, with abnormally low tides.[1] Currents are associated with approximately 11 unique sea-ice conditions and, from the time of freeze-up, Inuit note the role of currents in creating good ice conditions for hunting:

We know the new ice is usually bad at freeze-up. Usually, it is broken up by the currents, and starts [forming] again with new fresh ice that is in much better condition.

Lucassie Iqaluk, Inukjuak

Floe-edge ice breaks away in areas where currents are stronger than the wind during freeze-up; however, where the wind and currents are weak, ice builds continuously at the floe edge until spring.

Currents in northwestern Hudson Bay begin to gain strength in September, October, and November, when unconsolidated sea ice is forming. They are strongest in December, during the shortest days of the year, and remain strong until March. They strengthen again in spring when the volume of freshwater run-off increases as the melt begins. These stronger currents assist ice break-up in river mouths, helping separate ice from the shore. Currents weaken in the later stages of spring thaw, but regain strength by summer and contribute to rough waves on windy days.

Figure 3: Surface Current Activity and Changes in Hudson and James Bays

LEGEND:

→ General circulation

▨ Area of weakening currents

Foxe Basin

BAFFIN ISLAND

Repulse Bay

Wager Bay

Foxe Channel

Roes Welcome Sound

Southampton Island

Coral Harbour

Cape Dorset

Lake Harbour

Hudson Strait

Kazau River

Chesterfield Inlet

Rankin Inlet

Cape Jones

Whale Cove

Ivujivik

Salluit

Kangiqsujuaq

Akulivik

Chukotat River

Thlewiaza River

Arviat

Povungnituk

Povungnituk River

Kogaluc River

Seal River

Churchill

HUDSON BAY

Inukjuak

Churchill River

Umiujaq

Sanikiluaq

York Factory

York Landing

Nelson River

Shamattawa

Hayes River

Ft. Severn

Belcher Islands

Cape Henrietta Maria

Great Whale River

Kuujjuaraapik / Whapmagoostui

La Grande Reservoir

Severn River

Peawanuck

Winisk River

Chisasibi

JAMES BAY

Wemindji

Eastmain River

Attawapiskat River

Attawapiskat

Akimiski Island

Eastmain

Kashechewan

Ft. Albany

Rupert River

Albany River

Moosonee Moose Factory

Waskaganish

Lake Mistassini

Moose R.

N

0   100   200   300 km

© Hudson Bay Programme: Municipality of Sanikiluaq

Cartography: Michael J. Fisher, Edmonton, Alberta

Source: Hudson Bay Programme, *Traditional Ecological Knowledge of Environmental Changes in Hudson and James Bays, Part I.* (Ottawa: HBP, 1995), 35.

Inuit know the moon has a strong effect on tidal currents; they use this traditional knowledge to forecast weather, interpret environmental indicators, and determine animal behaviour. Hunters, for instance, know when it is time to look for beluga whales:

During winter, when the high tide comes, the beach ice will be saturated with water leaking through shoreline cracks. When the high tide and strong currents come, it is time to look for beluga whales because the winds will be strong and coming from the northwest. That is when you expect to see some beluga at the floe edge.

Noah Isaac, Salluit

They also know that a storm develops when the current acts *as if it has stopped knowing where it is supposed to go* during high tide. At this time, animals at the floe edge stop moving and are not seen anywhere.

Inuit and coastal Cree observe a *strong current period* (spring tides):

The strong current period we call ingiranituq *affects everything around us. It even affects the freshwater river system. The rivers will overflow with water during that time. There are two moon effects each month. When the moon is full we get very high tides and strong currents. It also happens during new moon. It never fails, and you will not notice strong currents any other time.*

Nala Nappaaluk, Kangiqsujuaq

When the strong currents are happening, it tells you that the floe edge has broken up, which means hunting will be much better on your next trip there. The [polynyas] will have much better edges because the overflow makes them nice and strong and smooth.

Peter Audlaluk, Ivujivik

The strength of the currents and variation of the tides decrease in the first moon quarter. Between first quarter and half moon, the force of the currents slowly increases; tidal action remains reasonably constant. At half moon, both the tides and the currents are at normal levels.

The currents build in strength after half moon, and variation between high and low tides begins to increase. By third quarter, tides are high and currents have strengthened. The current force continues to increase towards full moon, when the weather usually changes.[2] Strong winds frequently accompany the full moon, and animals are very active until maximum current force is reached two days after full moon. When areas of open water expand during full moon, more fox tracks are seen in the snow and more animals are sighted at the floe edge and in polynyas.

Currents sustain marine productivity in Hudson Bay:

Mussels eat sea bugs that go around with the current. They open their shells during high tides so they eat small sea bugs, even the micro-sized ones. Mussels living in areas where the currents are weak are very thin because there is less food in these areas. Sea-bottom organisms eat only with the help of the currents [and some] really rely on currents because they stay where they were born. Mussels that ... have just the right environment will be fatter because their foods move to them in larger numbers.

Charlie Arngak, Kangiqsujuaq; Lucassie Iqaluk, Inukjuak

Marine mammals, including beluga, ringed seal, harp seal, bearded seal, and walrus, depend on currents to feed and to travel. Sea birds such as mergansers, Arctic terns, and northern eiders also depend on currents for food:

The currents are the marine animals' access to [food]. Inuit also need the currents, and we are always watching the currents for hunting. Seals come and go with the currents. There would be no whales if there were no currents.

Peter Matte, Akulivik

When the currents are stronger so are the smaller sea organisms. Smaller birds also seem to feed more when the currents are strong. It seems that way with walrus, too. They are more visible when the currents are strong.

Donat Milortok, Repulse Bay

Some years we don't have access to walrus due to the ice. If it leaves early in summer then we have more walrus, but if there is too much ice they are scarce. It also depends on the current because, sometimes, if too much old ice from the north drifts towards Repulse Bay, walrus are scarce in the fall. The current strength varies each summer. Sometimes, it is stronger so the walrus are only about 65 kilometres away in fall, and at the floe edge in winter ... but if there is too much ice the walrus are scarce. The current has a major role with access.

John Kaunak, Repulse Bay; Jimmy Eetuk, Coral Harbour

The walrus in Wakeham Bay area stay only at the floe edge where [there are] currents in winter. It is rare to see a walrus where there is no current, at our floe edge, in wintertime.

Nala Nappaaluk, Kangiqsujuaq

Whales, seals, and walrus cover greater distances when the currents are strong in either their seasonal or their lunar cycle:

All sea mammals are able to travel further [and faster] with the help of currents. In fall ... places where there were no seals could have lots of seals when the currents come. All the animals in water seem to come alive when currents strengthen.

John Kaunak, Repulse Bay

The mammals are actually controlled by the current. In Ivujivik area, the whales like to travel into the current. They also go with the current, but they prefer to face it. Even in winter, they like to be in the current system. It is the other way around with seals. They will go with the current. The seals further out in the open sea are much thinner than those closer to the shoreline.

Peter Audlaluk, Ivujivik

... current animals always watch the current movements when they head towards Hudson Bay. Take, for example, beluga whales. When they are travelling to Hudson Bay they go along the shoreline. They stay very close to the shoreline, to avoid the stronger offshore current. When the current changes they go further offshore. Those whales will not show up during low tide, but they will when the current starts moving again.

Mark Kadjulik, Salluit

It is the same with whales in Wakeham Bay area. [They] start to move when the current is about to change direction, in its weakest movement at the highest or lowest point of the [flood and ebb] tides. You may wait for whales all day and there will be none while the high tide comes in. Then, the whales show up at the end of the day when the high tide is right at its highest level.

Nala Nappaaluk, Kangiqsujuaq

Sea ice

Sea ice is essential to Inuit, coastal Cree, and marine mammals in Hudson Bay. Inuit have always spiritually respected the sea ice as a living form with influence on the daily lives of both humans and animals. Their strong reliance on sea ice for travelling and hunting is reflected in their knowledge of its processes, characteristics, and annual cycles.[3]

Sea ice is used in many ways by marine mammals. Seals maintain large "caves" under the thick snow on the sea ice for birthing dens and spend much time on top of the ice during their annual moult. Both seals and walrus bask on sea ice once the days begin to lengthen. Polar bears in the Southampton Island area give birth and travel and hunt on sea ice. Its bottom surface provides habitat for numerous organisms in the marine food chain.

The formation of sea ice varies with weather and currents. Different ice conditions determine which sea mammals are present in winter, which areas can support hunting and travel, and the type of spring break-up. If, for example, the floe-edge ice doesn't break off during spring tides, the landfast ice will continue to expand and thicken, altering habitat for ringed seals, bearded seals, and eider ducks, in particular.

Inuit use distinct terms to describe each different ice condition through five stages of development. Seven ice conditions are linked directly to early ice formation; 25 are related to development of landfast ice; and 34 to ice developing from the floe edge, including those associated with marine currents and "ice joints" (figure 4). One is relevant only to spring, and four others occur only after spring break-up.

New sea ice forms during the first three stages, following the same general freezing process whether it is forming early in the season, during the development of landfast ice, or in association with marine currents and ice joints.

Stage 1:   Early ice formation—shoreline to land points in inlets, bays, and peninsulas

In most areas of Hudson Bay new sea ice starts to form during October and November.

Qainguniq and *qainguk* result from slush, formed under colder air temperatures offshore, that is washed ashore by the wind, where it freezes as beach ice at the high-water mark. It remains on the shoreline until it melts in spring. Similarly, *qinuk* and *minguirniq* (slush ice) form along shorelines and at the floe edge if snow is either falling or blowing onshore. When new ice forms from slush in narrow water bodies, like inlets, it is called *qiqngurusirtuk*. Although harder than *qinuk*, *qiqngurusirtuk* is still soft and unreliable for travel.

Akgutitak and *akgutinik* apply to a slushy mixture of ice and snow that freezes into flexible ice and moves with the waves. It starts forming along the shoreline and extends farther from the land when winds are blowing in to the shore. It is not safe to walk on.

Sikulirutit, qaiquit, tullukkalait, and *putatak* are new ice, freshly frozen from part saltwater and part freshwater along shorelines and within inlets. High tide will float it and winds can blow it offshore in broken pieces. When there is no wind, currents also move it. Seals like to be on this ice.

On a calm day, very thin layers of new ice called *sikuak* and *agutitaat* can form, often attaching to the shoreline or other ice. When it thickens, *sikuak* supports very good breathing holes for seals. Once inlets are frozen over, new ice called *sikutak* (new ice that forms from *sikuak*), *ukiurjait,* and *tuvasak* forms. *Sikutait* is solid ice in small inlets or bays formed before the landfast ice starts developing. *Sikuliak* is newly formed ice with no snow on top; it is thinner than old ice, but safe to walk or travel on.

Stage 2:   Development of landfast ice

Very thin ice forms from *sikutait*, and from the edge of shoreline ice, when landfast ice begins to develop. As the landfast ice extends farther from the shoreline, floe leads and the floe edge form. The floe leads open and close repeatedly, and the landfast ice never stops forming as long as temperatures remain at or below freezing.

Maturing *sikuliak* becomes *tuvak*, a landfast ice that stays frozen in the bay and coastal areas and becomes solid ice attached to the shorelines. The last ice to leave an area after break-up, it moves only when the snow melts and shoreline cracks start expanding in spring.

Uiguak usually forms as smooth, solid ice when wind blows from the landfast ice. It will meet *akgutitak*, a rough, slushy, unsafe ice that attaches and extends from the floe edge when winds are blowing in to the shore. *Sikuliak* forms when *uiguak* and *akgutinik* meet and freeze solid. Thin crystals called *kangutik* and *kanijuk* form on top of *sikuliak*.

Figure 4: Effects of Currents, Spring Tides, and Wind on Sea Ice

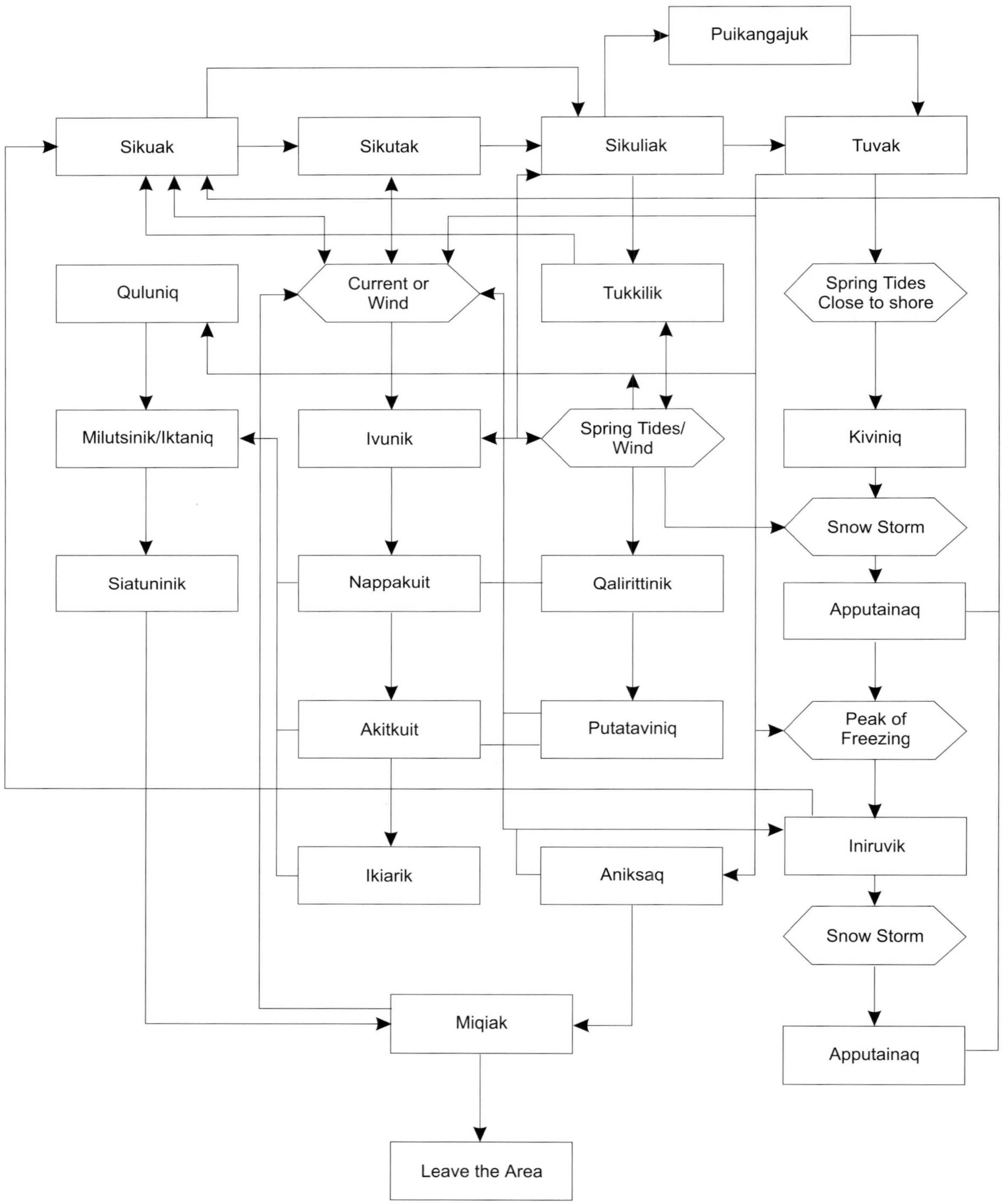

Source: Hudson Bay Programme, *Traditional Ecological Knowledge of Environmental Changes in Hudson and James Bays, Part II.* (Ottawa: HBP, 1995), 35.

Napakkait, quliqiaq, napakutak, and *napakkuit* refer to ice only three to six millimetres thick when broken by the forces of winds, currents, or waves. Some pieces go down and others go up, freezing into ice sheets separated by open water. *Ikiarik* forms when one piece of solid ice is pushed on top of another during a wind storm or spring tides.

Aniksaq describes a large piece of solid ice with no cracks that has been broken off from the floe edge either by strong winds or currents or after moving ice collided with landfast ice. *Putataviniq* and *putatait* refer to an older piece of ice, separated from other ice by currents, on which new ice *(sikuliak)* has formed. It will remain thicker and higher than the new ice if it doesn't break up again.

Tukkilik and *ajukraq* are cracks that occur between two islands or pieces of land when there is water under the ice. Because the cracks shift every day, the ice that forms in *tukkiliit* (plural) is thin and seals use the cracks to make breathing holes. *Tukkiliit* deformed by the pressure of high and low tides are called *quluniq* and *siqkutiniq.* Ice on both sides of the cracks is pushed upwards—usually when the sea ice is preparing for break-up—and a new thin layer forms underneath.

When the weight of high-tide water that has risen up through cracks depresses the ice and snow surface, the depression, usually formed near shorelines, is called *kiviniq.*

Polynyas (areas of open water) are of great importance to hunters and to various sea mammals and eider ducks, which depend on them for access to air and for shelter and feeding. Inuit use specific terms to describe different characteristics of polynyas.

Pullait are air pockets with a very thin layer of "false ice"—*apputainaq*—covering open water. One type is formed by air bubbles from eider ducks diving for food through openings underneath the ice during early freeze-up. The other type is made by current-formed air bubbles.

Puikkangajuk is ice that forms in polynyas during stormy weather or currents. Where the current is strongest, ice called *aukani* and *aukajuk* forms.

Stage 3: Development of floe-edge ice

While many ice types described in the "early ice formation" and "development of landfast ice" stages also occur at the floe edge, the development of floe-edge ice is particularly affected by currents and winds.[4]

Aulaniq and *ukkiutjait* describe newly formed ice continuously moving in currents beyond the floe edge. Pieces of ice moving as a group in the current are called *siatuninik.*

When the force of strong currents and moving ice causes thin pieces of ice to pile up on one another the resulting ice is called *qalirittinik*. *Ivunik* is rough, scrambled ice of varying thickness formed when moving ice collides with the floe edge and piles up. *Akitkuit, aqiqakuit,* and *akkiqaninkuit* form when ice is broken up by strong currents or waves colliding against the floe edge and the broken ice is submerged, allowing new ice to form on top.

When large areas of sea ice form, as in eastern Hudson Bay, "ice joints" occur along the thinner edge of what was the floe edge. To keep the ice flexible, these joints—*iniruviit*—open and close continuously like a hinge during high and low tides, but they do not shift sideways. During spring tides, and as soon as the temperature rises a few degrees, the ice in joints and larger leads breaks off at the point of least resistance. *Qullupiaq* and *piquniq* are new cracks that form in different directions when ice collides at the floe edge. The force of impact creates cracks in both the solid ice and the incoming ice. New cracks covered with snow are called *apputainaq*—"false ice"—because there is no ice underneath the snow. These cracks will often freeze solid within a few days.

Qamait and *piqurniq* form when the pressure that causes ice to break pushes the broken ice upwards. Seals use them during winter months. *Milutsinik* and *iktaniq* are formed at the floe edge when snow-soaked water freezes. Unsafe in current areas, this ice is avoided by hunters and animals.

Akirataviniq refers to ice broken up by strong currents or high winds.

Stage 4: Spring cracks

Although the thickness of sea ice differs each year depending on weather conditions, most sea ice in Hudson Bay melts completely and new ice forms annually.

Ice joints are the first breaking points in spring. Later, the cracks between land points, where ringed and bearded seals have wintered, get wider—*ajuraq*—and as ice starts to break away in them the landfast ice begins to break up.

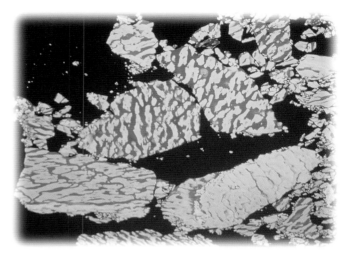

Stage 5: After break-up from spring to early summer

Tuvak breaks into big ice packs called *aniksaat*—large pieces of floating solid ice with no cracks. Separated from the floe edge by strong currents or wind, *aniksaat* can be further broken up by currents or wind.

Wind and currents start gathering ice packs together to move in to the shorelines once the landfast ice breaks up.

Brownish-coloured pack ice called *anakluk* is ice from shorelines and sandy, shallow water or ice that turned over after the current or strong winds broke it from the floe edge. It often originates in southern Hudson Bay and James Bay.

Thick pack ice from north Hudson Bay called *miqiaq*—"moulting ice"—often crowds areas so there is no open water in sight. It will stay near the shoreline until it is clean, and during this time it *acts as if it has a mind of its own* because no wind, tides, or currents will move it. Inuit have often seen *miqiaat* suddenly move out heading into strong winds.

Arctic multi-year ice enters Foxe Basin through Fury and Hecla Strait, and on occasion has travelled as far south as Arviat. Multi-year ice in Hudson Strait flows west, following the north shore to a point west of Cape Dorset, where it reverses and travels in east-flowing currents again.

Hudson Bay food web

Cree and Inuit observe and respect a natural order of relationships connecting the largest animals to the smallest organisms. Residents of the Hudson Bay bioregion identified 138 animal and 36 plant types: 4 types of marine plants, 10 different sea-bottom animals, 11 sea mammal species, 6 species of marine fish, 14 sea birds, 7 ducks, 9 waterfowl, 21 freshwater fish, 30 land birds, 16 fur-bearing animals, 14 land animals, 17 types of berries, and 15 plant species. The seasonal availability of food affects the diets of almost all animals—including humans—that travel or reside in Hudson Bay.

Small shoreline birds feed on tiny freshwater organisms, and larger sea birds eat small marine organisms. Small organisms also depend on the larger species. Certain species of shrimp, for instance, are known as the sea's "cleaners" because they eat any decaying matter. In the open-water season, Inuit dispose of sea mammal carcasses so the shrimp have the food they need and can, in turn, support the many fish, birds, and sea mammals, including sculpins, Arctic char, Arctic cod, Arctic terns, common eiders, black guillemots, sea gulls, seals, and bowheads, that eat them.

Figure 5, drawn from information provided on seasonal foods in Cree and Inuit diets and the foods that the animals in those diets eat, illustrates some of these inter-species relationships.

Seasonal foods

Cree and Inuit regard natural foods as a gift of life from the animals. Their traditional diets depend on the seasonal availability of animals, cultural preference, and geographical variation in the Hudson Bay ecosystem, as illustrated in figures 6 and 7.

Belcher Islands Inuit

Ringed seal, bearded seal, common eider, and sea-bottom animals (i.e., mussels, sea urchins, sea cucumbers, clams, and starfish) are dietary staples in the Belcher Inuit diet. They are supplemented by other foods that reside in the archipelago either year-round or seasonally (figure 6).

This includes local fish and reindeer populations, which are eaten only at certain times of the year.[5] Reindeer, for example, are consumed during the coldest part of the year and from the first of May to mid-September, when Inuit travel and live throughout Flaherty and Tukarak islands, but not when females are calving from the end of March to early May, when males are rutting in September and October, or when land and ice are freezing in November and early December. Various fish species like Arctic char, Arctic cod, whitefish, and sculpin also supplement the Inuit diet, but none are consumed during early spring when sea and freshwater ice are very thick.

Early spring provides the least variety in the Belcher Inuit diet because a number of foods are simply not available. It is also the time when build-up and extension of solid ice reduces the number of polynyas supporting the eider population and makes it difficult for seals to keep all of their breathing holes open.

Like the Cree and other Inuit, Belcher Islands Inuit look forward to the arrival of birds in spring. After a long winter, it signals seasonal and dietary changes as Canada geese and Arctic char become staples, supplemented with seal, sculpin, and cranberries. When the whales come into open areas of water, eagerly anticipated whale skin (*mattaq*) and air-dried whale meat (*nikkuk*) will also be added.

The larger sea mammals—beluga whale and walrus—are widely shared as "community foods" at the time of harvest. During winter, reindeer are also a community food.

Figure 5: Hudson Bay Food Web

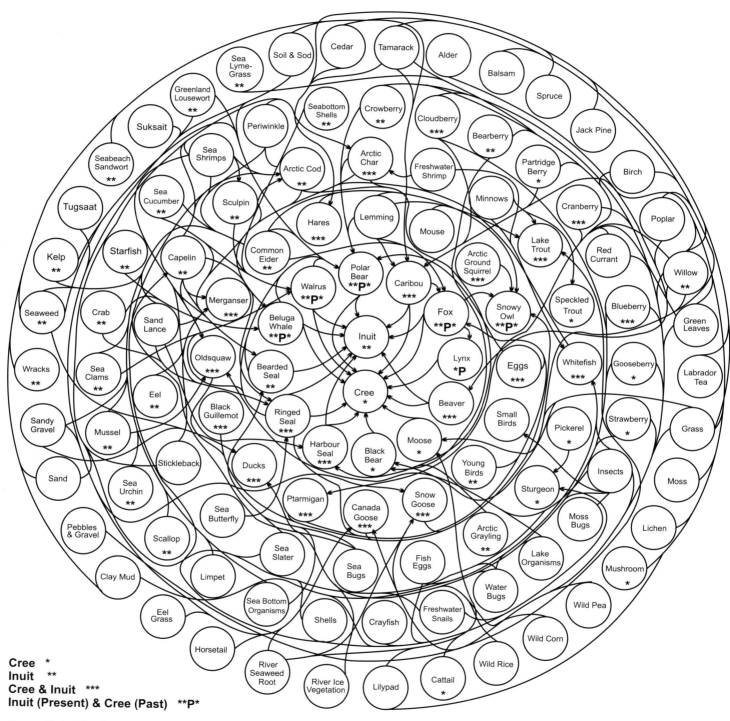

Source: Hudson Bay Programme, *Traditional Ecological Knowledge of Environmental Changes in Hudson and James Bays, Part I.* (Ottawa: HBP, 1995), 26.

Figure 6: Seasonal Foods of Belcher Islands Inuit

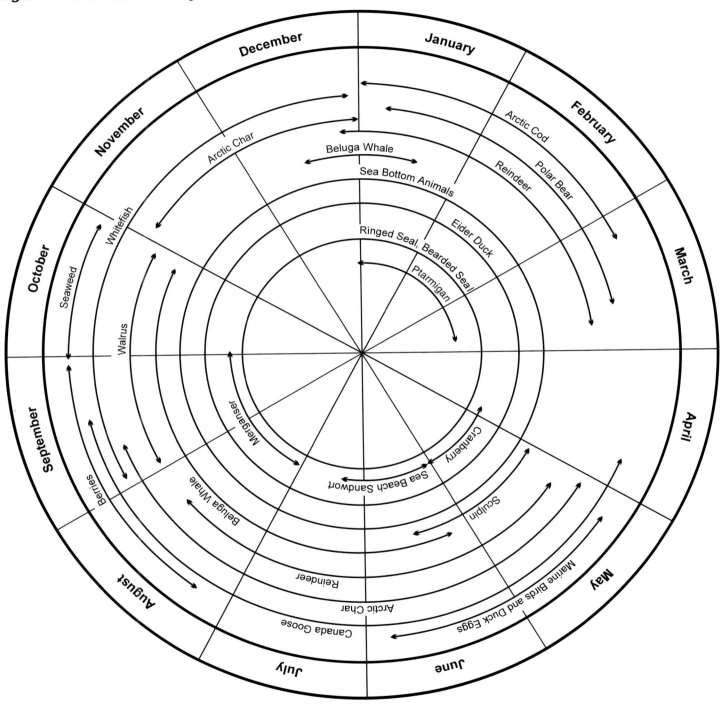

Source: Hudson Bay Programme, *Traditional Ecological Knowledge of Environmental Changes in Hudson and James Bays, Part I.* (Ottawa: HBP, 1995), 28.

21

James Bay Cree

A variety of foods enriches the traditional diet of Cree and reflects a number of activities in the annual cycle (figure 7). A Wemindji Elder elaborates:

I will start with fall, and the fall goose hunt, in the month of September. This is when the goose hunt started and it went into the month of October. We did not hunt in the same place every year.

I am talking about the past, not the present. People went out on their traplines much sooner than they do now. They were out in their territory before the cold weather set in and ... the first thing they did was fish. [At the same time], *the implements to be used for winter were prepared.*

In October, they started their trapping activities. ... The trapping of most animals stopped in March when the fur quality started to change but the otter and muskrat trapping did not stop until it was time to start the trip back to the Post [in] *June. In March, the lynx was also still trapped because the fur was still good quality. At the end of May, all the traps were gathered.*

Today, people stop their trapping activities much sooner because the animal reproduction cycle is being taken into more consideration than before.

Now, the spring goose hunt goes on from the end of April until the 20th of May. Before, both the Canada and snow goose were around longer and the height of migration was when they started to come at the same time. The length of the goose season was determined by looking at the size of the eggs. If the eggs were small then the hunt would be long, but if the eggs were large the goose migration would be short. I know this for a fact. I keep track of it.

When the goose migration was over at the end of May, the red-throated loons came into the bay. They would come in flocks by the middle of the month. The loons and Arctic terns flew north at the same time, so if you saw the terns then you would

know that the loons were not far behind. This was how the people knew when to expect the loons. It is still the case today.

In June, as soon as there was open water, the fish nets would be set. This activity continued throughout the summer. In the month of August, the fish started to go up the rivers to feed close along the shore.

In September, the fall goose hunt began. But, today, the goose goes south earlier than it did, so the fall hunt is much shorter. Before, large flocks would fly south in October when the weather started to get cold. These geese would be nice and fat, and the weather was cold enough so they could be kept frozen outdoors. This was how long the goose would stay north long ago. Today, the geese have all gone south at the beginning of October.

It is very different now than how I remember it in the past. I just wanted to mention the start and end of the various harvesting times for different wildlife. I will not talk too much about the past because the hunting times were basically the same for all of us.

John Matches, Wemindji

Notes

1. The number of cracks that form between land points also depends upon current force.

2. The strong current period is not as effective when a low pressure system occurs at the same time.

3. Sanikiluaq Elders Advisory Meeting 1. 1993. Unpublished transcript. HBP: Sanikiluaq. The sea-ice cycles were organized from a list of names provided in the first set of meetings. The stages and distinct types of ice associated with each cycle explained in this section of the book were verified by Inuit hunters and Elders during the second set of meetings.

4. Floe edges never stay in one place (any time of the day, week, month, or year). Solid ice is continuously broken off by moving ice, and new ice forms from where the break occurs.

5. Not native to the Belcher Islands, reindeer were introduced in 1978 as a food supplement and now provide an important source of food; they are hunted, not herded.

Figure 7: Seasonal Foods of Western James Bay Cree

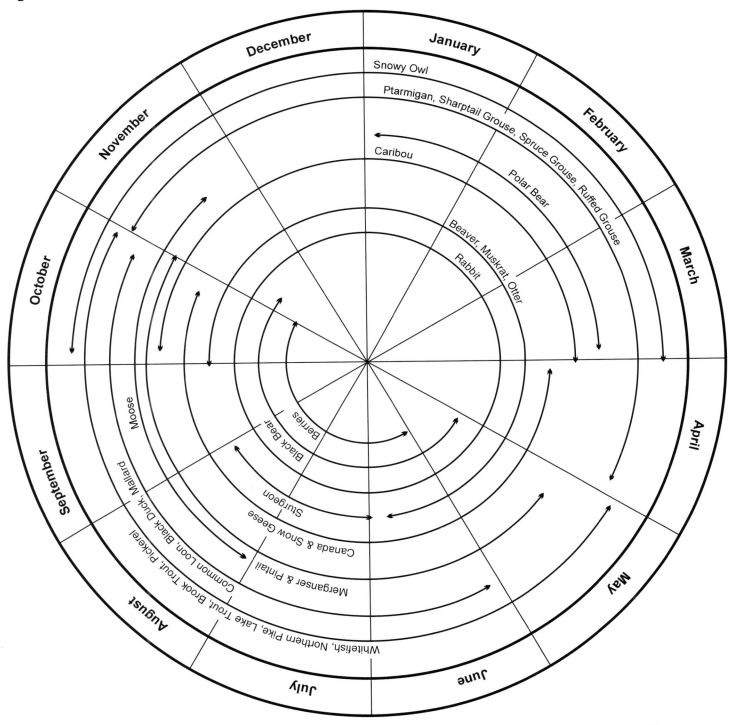

Source: Hudson Bay Programme, *Traditional Ecological Knowledge of Environmental Changes in Hudson and James Bays, Part I.* (Ottawa: HBP, 1995), 30.

"In our traditional knowledge, when you use the animals according to their purpose, they will always prosper and reproduce themselves as you need them. We can never believe it when we're told the animals are decreasing because we know how the animals and environment work up here. We also know any living being will cease to exist when the time comes."

Environmental Change and Its Significance to Inuit and Cree

The correct interpretation of environmental change has often meant the difference between life and death to traditional Hudson Bay Cree and Inuit. As hunters and trappers, they are skilled in recognizing natural indicators of change and systematically interpret the consequences of those changes. They watch the way lakes, rivers, and sea water freeze to determine where fish, birds, and sea mammals will be found during the winter months and to predict how the ice will break up in spring. They know that animal fat content varies seasonally, and they are not concerned if animals are thin when they *are supposed to be thin.*

Indigenous knowledge is acquired collectively, through learning, following the advice of Elders, and interacting in natural surroundings according to traditional beliefs and practices. Recognizing their place in the Hudson Bay bioregion, Cree and Inuit understand that everything from the smallest insect to the stars has a purpose and must be respected. They know that, when altered by humans, natural systems and everything connected to them do not function as before.

A long history of adapting to change enables Inuit and Cree to define types of change. Natural and cyclical change is anticipated; humans try to adapt by watching animals and by listening to or recalling Elders' explanations of what has gone before. Sudden or unexpected natural change causes problems for both humans and animals. Unnatural change that introduces something new or foreign to the system can force major adjustments by entire communities.

Environmental change provoked by human activities has had significant effects on the lives of Cree and Inuit in the Hudson Bay bioregion.

In 1957, before the Churchill-Nelson hydroelectric development was begun, the York Factory Cree, a traditional coastal people, were relocated inland to York Landing and compelled to adapt to a very small area of land.[1] Upstream damming has had additional impacts on this relocated community. Today, residents associate their loss of livelihood, health, language, and culture directly with their loss of traditional resources. Fred Beardy, of York Landing, expresses their feelings when he says, "when the system is healthy you are healthy. When the system is polluted it kills you slowly. The damming has destroyed our way of life."

The western James Bay Cree have also lost traditional territories and witnessed major changes in their natural surroundings.[2] They are encountering the cumulative effects of regional industrial activity:

> *Our people in the Moose River area have perhaps had the longest experience in seeing the effect of hydro developments. The first dam was constructed around 1914, and construction of a number of dams continued to about 1960. During that 50-year period the people had no say about what happened at all. The dams were never negotiated ... the [Cree] people only found out what was happening when they actually saw a dam being built right in their trapping land. We also found out that what makes it even worse is that they put in a road when they build those projects. After the road is in, then they come in and start cutting the trees down and looking for other things like minerals. Hunters also start coming in from the south. So hydroelectric development brings a lot of other effects that are just as bad as—perhaps worse than—the dam itself.*
>
> John Turner, Moose Factory

Cree in the eastern James Bay region note that rates and impacts of change have been much greater since Hydro-Québec started damming, diking, and flooding rivers in the 1970s.[3] Family hunting territories have been flooded, river travel routes either submerged or drained of water, camps vandalized, and traditional sacred sites destroyed. They feel their land and their lives have been invaded:

> *All of a sudden somebody from down south did some work in our territory. We didn't know what was going on. Nobody told us. We saw signs. The Elders told us something was going to happen.*

Culture shock I call it. They dammed the river. A lot of work. So suddenly it hurt a lot of our Elders. The lifestyle changed. The health changed. All these new things: civilization, money—lots of it. We could buy anything: food from the store, skidoos to go anywhere you want to go, cars, the pleasures of life—go on holidays. We didn't know what we were doing. We couldn't even go inland on the lakes or rivers like before. Everything was motorized. We couldn't walk. We'd walk a few feet and take a rest. We got lazy. Spoiled. That's how it is now. Our health is gone. But we're slowly bringing it back to our kids.

Edward Tapiatic, Chisasibi

Eastern James Bay Cree still pursue a traditional life based on natural foods because they believe that *to heal, you have to go back to the land and eat the food.* The seasonal diet of coastal Cree, however, has been affected by a decline in fish populations and a shift in the migration routes of Canada and snow geese, and the diet of inland Cree has been affected by a decline of fish and small game.

The sturgeon is affected along with other species of fish. It is on the decline, more so than at the beginning of the flooding. There were plenty of fish before all this happened. Now it is a different story. There are less lake fish in the hunting territories. It is the same story with the birds, especially the willow ptarmigan. There used to be plenty of them during winter.

William Fireman, Chisasibi

Every year when inland Cree return to their territories they witness more change. Eastmain, Wemindji, and Chisasibi Cree can no longer eat fish from some rivers because they are contaminated with mercury. Spawning sites and migration routes for several species, including whitefish, sturgeon, dore, and pike, have been ruined or no longer exist. Debris and sediment building up at river mouths prevent coastal Cree from fishing with nets.

Hydroelectric development and logging activities have destroyed habitat and altered environmental conditions favourable to small game. Once a winter dietary staple, ptarmigan haven't been seen in the Wemindji area for ten years, and rabbits are no longer plentiful.

The main flyway for Canada and snow geese has shifted to the east, possibly because of habitat changes in coastal wetland areas and the creation, by reservoirs, of new inland shoreline and marsh habitat. Although berries still grow and fully ripen in the interior, plant life that geese and ducks feed on in the coastal areas is greatly diminished.

In eastern Hudson Bay, the proposed development of the Grand Baleine hydroelectric complex has been of grave recent concern.[4] The Cree predict that their land and waters will be destroyed:

If more dams are built it will affect us in a negative way. The water will not freeze and everything will be destroyed including the fish that come from the north every year. We are already noticing a difference in the fish. The Arctic char and trout used to be large. If more rivers are dammed, then there will be more destruction because this kind of activity affects animals, fish, and all water life. This is what we expect will happen; the rivers will be contaminated and polluted. There will be mercury in the water at a very high level. Our land will be destroyed and, once the land is destroyed, it can't be exchanged or brought back to the way it was.

John Petegumskum, Whapmagoostui

The Inuit predict the environmental effects will be widespread:

Those Hydro people tell us there is no problem nor any kind of danger from the project they are working on, but rivers and streams flow to the Hudson Bay so everything will be affected. The fish spawn along the smaller streams which flow into larger river systems which flow into the sea. The effects won't be just in Manitounuk Sound because marine animals travel all over the place. Hydro is saying the effects will not go far in the marine water, but the discharge system will be very strong, and we have sea current systems which can carry things further than they think.

Peter Matte, Akulivik; Lucassie Iqaluk, Inukjuak

In Hudson Strait, mining activities near Salluit and Kangiqsujuaq have contaminated the water system and affected the terrestrial environment.[5] Fish and marine shellfish (e.g., clams) in coastal areas near asbestos mines have been found to contain contaminants. Abandoned equipment and materials from the Deception Bay mine are corroding, and contaminants pass into a lake where char, whitefish, and other fish feed.[6] People have seen severely malnourished fish trying to swim when they are barely alive; in comparison, fish living farther away from the mine are large and healthy.

A tributary of the Salluit River will be dammed, obstructing migrating Arctic char, to support newly begun mining activities. Construction of communities, roads, and bridges will require displacement of large volumes of earth and will directly affect fish and other wildlife by altering their feeding areas and travel routes.

Northwestern Hudson Bay residents note that caribou, which are not intimidated by mining activity, migrate very close to work camps and may feed in contaminated areas; they wonder about a link between mine tailings and the high rate of cancer-related deaths among Elders since 1990.[7] Disappearance of wildlife from the area may also be a result of mining:

We moved to Rankin Inlet in 1957. There weren't very many people and buildings then. Before there was a lot of fishing activity on the shores in front of the bay, but there is none of that now. This is directly related to the mine tailings that went to the bay. There used to be numerous ringed seals on the bay ice in spring but they are gone too. What also contributed to the fish and seals disappearing is the underground mine blasting that occurred because wildlife have sensitive hearing mechanisms.

Matilda Sulurayok, Arviat

In addition to these specific impacts of industrial development in the Hudson Bay bioregion, Cree and Inuit have observed changes in the atmosphere, weather, currents, sea-water salinity, shorelines, river systems, and fish and wildlife.

Atmosphere

When I was a young man, the only thing that made the sky look different was natural smog from the south winds. It came from the burning trees way down south. In today's weather, very dirty things are falling from the sky.

Nala Nappaaluk, Kangiqsujuaq

A change in the colour of the sky and the emergence of a high altitude haze have been observed in all coastal areas of the Hudson Bay system.[8] In the early 1990s, eastern Hudson Bay and Hudson Strait Inuit found it affected seasonal processes in winter and spring and these, in turn, affected summer weather.

Eastern James Bay Elders find the natural taste of land animals and plants changing and associate this with *strange smells in the air like gasoline.* Elders in western James Bay and Hudson Strait also attribute atmospheric change to a growing amount of air pollution:

You can see very well that those haze-like things in the sky are the work of man-made problems. It's coming from air pollution like cars and airplanes. Even those big planes are one of the polluters. In the old days, it was nice, warm and rained when it had to, but these days, you get falling snow instead of rain in the spring. The dirty smoke or smog affects the weather very much.

Mark Kadjulik, Salluit

The sky in eastern Hudson Bay has become light blue and a shade of pale yellow in the 1990s. In the past, it was darker blue and Inuit could look directly at the sun even when there were no clouds. Today, the sunlight hurts the eyes, and people are advised to wear sunglasses.

Hudson Strait Inuit describe the sun as having a *strong burning effect on human skin,* and it has burnt the faces of Belcher Islands hunters, a phenomenon considered very unusual. Between 1990 and 1993 the sun's heat seemed to change. When a white, misty haze in the higher atmosphere screened the sun, both northwestern Hudson Bay and Hudson Strait Inuit observed that insects and vegetation did not thrive and the sun was less effective in melting the snow and ice.

The people of western James Bay suspect that changing atmospheric conditions are responsible for a change in the colour, composition, and taste of snow, which when melted obviously contains dirt particles. Community representatives in eastern Hudson Bay, Hudson Strait, and northwestern Hudson Bay attribute changes in snow composition to changing weather systems. Both eastern James Bay Cree and Hudson Strait Inuit report on the transport of pollutants:

Two springs ago, we noticed the snow was covered with particles from a black substance that was visible to the eye. It was like a black powder. It started in early spring when there was a south wind, and it was snowing at the time. It was really noticeable out on the ice, where the snow was black after the snowfall. You could also see something black floating when the snow melted on top of the ice. This stuff came from the air. They thought it came from the tire fire down in Montreal. It must have been in the atmosphere for a while before it came down with the snow.

Jimmy Rupert, Chisasibi

There was a dark smog that was not natural once. It was man-made smog that turned the sky dark in broad daylight. The sunlight was a reddish colour, and you could look directly at the sun because it was not bright anymore. That dark black smog affected our drinking water and the food animals eat. It also completely ruined our hunting tents because everything turned black with soot falling from the sky ... people in our community tried to find out what it was. At that time, they were told tires burning. It was an accident that happened down in Ontario.

Inuit hunters, Northern Quebec

Weather

Both Cree and Inuit use environmental indicators to interpret weather patterns, forecast conditions, and predict seasonal events. In the early 1990s people in both cultures were finding that some environmental indicators that had been used for generations did not coincide with the existing weather system. Moreover, people in Hudson Strait, northwestern Hudson Bay, and eastern James Bay were less confident in their predictions:

Even if we try to predict what it is going to be like tomorrow ... the environmental indication isn't what the Elders said it would be. Sometimes, it is still true but sometimes it isn't. In the past, when they said, "it's going to be like this tomorrow," it was. But our weather and environment are changing so our knowledge isn't true all the time now. We're being told [in Hudson Strait] that maybe if we put January, February, or March one month behind, our knowledge of weather would be more accurate because the weather in those months isn't the same anymore.

Lucassie Arragutainaq, Sanikiluaq

We cannot make predictions anymore. We don't know if the water is going to freeze or not. We used

In the same way that there is reason for good, clear weather, there is also reason for rain. Hence, good weather should be balanced with rainy and stormy weather if the environment is to function properly. All the weather conditions complement each other because rain, thunder, snow, and wind are all useful. Although many people may desire good weather all the time, it cannot occur if the world is going to continue surviving.

Inuk hunter, Hudson Strait

Since the 1940s, weather in northwestern Hudson Bay has become highly variable. There used to be more clear, calm days, winters were colder, and low temperatures persisted longer. By the early 1990s, weather changes were quick, unexpected, and difficult to predict. Blizzards, for example, would occur on clear days in the Chesterfield Inlet area, but on days when environmental indicators suggested a blizzard, it would not materialize.

Residents of Southampton Island observe different lake-ice conditions, a result of snow falling before freshwater freezes and creating a slush from which ice forms. Also, when the snow melts and then freezes over the ground or over a thin layer of snow, land animals, including young Arctic hare and ptarmigan, have difficulty foraging for food.

The small bird population has been affected by spring weather changes and has declined significantly. In the early 1990s, unseasonable cold during spring and summer in Chesterfield Inlet, Southampton Island, and Repulse Bay allowed little vegetation growth and no growth of some types of berries. Subsequently, caribou overgrazed some areas. Also, mosquito populations in the Repulse Bay area declined.

Black flies have migrated from the tree line into the Whale Cove area, where the snow melts earlier than in the past. In Arviat, the snow is gone by May but blizzards of snow and rain can occur in June.[9] Farther north, formerly permanent snowfields now melt in the summer.

In western Hudson Bay, Elders traditionally based their seasonal predictions of weather conditions and patterns on spring weather. Even though the actual melting of snow occurs at a much faster rate in the Fort Severn area, spring is getting colder, summers are shorter, fall freeze-up occurs earlier, and winter is becoming longer.

to know what was going to happen at certain seasons but, with all the changes in the climate and the different qualities of water, we can't make those predictions anymore.

Helen Atkinson, Chisasibi

Traditional Inuit and Cree rely on their understanding of various seasonal and weather conditions to obtain food. They appreciate the complexity of weather. Elders of southern Hudson Strait say that clear, calm weather needs to be balanced with stormy weather and that systematic changes in weather patterns take about ten years to occur:

In contrast, warmer temperatures have shortened winter in western James Bay. The ice in naturally flowing rivers is not as thick and some inland lakes now freeze for a shorter time. The taste of snow and rainwater has changed and melted snow no longer quenches the thirst.

Sudden shifts in the wind are also occurring:

We were sitting in the blind hunting Canada geese when my father mentioned about changes in the weather. The weather that day was calm and the wind kept changing direction. This mystified my father because, he says, long ago, the wind used to blow from the same direction for 12 days. Now, he notices the difference. Some days the wind changes to every direction.

Gilbert Soloman, Fort Albany

In eastern James Bay, spring used to last longer. In the early 1990s, the fall weather changes quickly and is warm, then very cold, within minutes. The cold weather arrives earlier, but lakes freeze later. The amount of snowfall has increased.

Flooding large tracts of land in inland eastern James Bay has increased the area of ice cover significantly, reducing local temperatures. Unused to the cold environment, animals suffer and leave. The areas with reservoirs no longer provide suitable winter habitat for beaver and muskrat, for as water levels are artificially lowered, their lodges are left sitting high, dry, and intensely cold. Fluctuating water levels also create precarious travelling conditions for moose, caribou, and Cree; lives have been lost crossing thin or unsupported ice on rivers and reservoirs.

Since 1984, April and May winds in the Belcher Islands have blown mostly from the north, reducing the size of Canada geese flocks, slowing the spring melt, and contributing to the spring and summer cooling trend in eastern Hudson Bay. At one time Akulivik had nice, calm weather for weeks, when warm clouds stayed for days, but by 1992 the warm clouds were present for only a day or so at a time. Between 1989 and 1993, constant cold temperatures from mid-December to early April extended the freezing period, making ice thicker and snow deeper and delaying the spring thaw.

A cooling trend has been observed in the Hudson Strait area over the past several years. Whereas spring and early summer used to be warm, cold winter weather now returns following a March or April warm spell and persists into May, June, and July. Some insect populations are declining; others are disappearing. Late melting of snow and ice extends their cooling influence, affecting the predictability and stability of summer weather systems.

The timing of the fall freeze-up in Hudson Strait has not changed, but the sea ice freezes faster than it did in the past and its quality has deteriorated in some areas because more slush ice develops during early freezing. A new freezing and melting cycle in the fall makes the snow too icy to be used for snow house construction during early winter.

Currents, polynyas, and sea ice

Marine animals depend on currents for travel and access to their food sources; birds depend on currents for feeding; and Inuit rely on currents for hunting. In eastern Hudson Bay, Inuit have observed change over 20 years that appears related to currents weakening, and the effects—extended sea-ice cover and reduced habitat for eider ducks—are of concern:

The ice between the Belcher, King George, and Sleeper islands now freezes over completely so people can travel to those places in winter which they couldn't do before. Also, east of Tukarak Island, the ice usually never stops moving back and forth because the currents are very strong there. But, since the winter of 1991, the ice in that area has been freezing solid which is causing the eider ducks to suffer a lot, and die in large numbers during the coldest months of the year.

Joanassie Arragutainaq, Sanikiluaq

Between the 1920s and 1970s the "ice bridge" between the Belcher Islands and the eastern Hudson Bay mainland occasionally froze by late February or early March (figure 8). In the 1970s, it began to freeze earlier and by the late 1980s started freezing as soon as the early freezing season began (figure 9). During the 1950s, 35 polynyas were open all winter in the Belcher Islands archipelago; in the 1960-70s, 13, and in the early 1990s, only 3.

Since the late 1980s, landfast ice in the Lake Harbour, Ivujivik, and Salluit areas has been extending farther into Hudson Strait. In the early 1990s, it froze over completely in areas where Inuit traditionally hunted seals and walrus:

In the Lake Harbour area, the ice didn't freeze completely between Big Island and south Baffin Island during winter. It now freezes over every year. The polynyas now freeze completely very early in the season, and the floe edge is further away. Also, the floe-edge ice is not breaking anymore, even in strong current periods ... Lake Harbour hunters don't go to the floe edge anymore, because it's so far away. In spring, the ice is not safe between the floe edge and mainland because it starts melting before breaking away. In the old days, the ice used to break away in June but since it began completely freezing over between Big Island and south Baffin Island, the ice is not even broken up at the beginning of July. In 1992, it broke away in mid-July.

Mikidjuk Kolola, Lake Harbour

A large recurring polynya used by Ivujivik and Salluit sea-ice hunters also started to freeze over in the 1980s, and in the early 1990s it no longer opens during spring tides:

The ice used to move around between the mainland and [Digges Island] in winter time but now it freezes over, and the floe edge is past the islands. Also, the ice used to break into pieces in polynyas, but it hasn't been doing that over the last ten years.

Peter Audlaluk, Ivujivik

Weaker currents bring fewer ice packs, which may be a reason for fewer polar bears in the Ivujivik area. In summer, the currents by Ivujivik and Salluit also appear to be weaker: there are no longer large waves on calm days (except preceding a storm), and changing current lines are no longer visible on the water's surface.

In the Cape Dorset area, the currents aren't weakening, but colder air temperatures are causing thin ice to form in open water areas at a much faster rate in recent years. Residents of Kangiqsujuaq also haven't observed currents weakening, but noted that the polynya near Anivak was freezing over in early winter.

In northwestern Hudson Bay, Inuit know the currents have weakened in Roes Welcome Sound because it is now possible to cross them during summer's spring tides. In 1992, a large polynya that seldom froze in January began freezing over in November and December.

Elders in the Arviat area have also observed a reduction in current movement. The combined effect of rising land—three new islands have emerged—and reduced river flow has contributed to currents *vanishing* and is a reason why there are fewer walrus and beluga in the area.[10]

The cause for currents weakening in eastern Hudson Bay and Hudson Strait is not known. Inuit know, however, that rivers are an important part of the Hudson Bay current system and have observed how reduced river flow affects currents in localized areas. They question, therefore, whether hydro development on three of the system's largest rivers has, over 30-40 years, significantly altered water flowing to the bay and contributed to weakening currents.

The regional maps for Hudson Strait and eastern Hudson Bay show tidal and surface current activity in the main areas where study participants identified currents weakening (figures 10 and 11; see also figure 3, page 12).

Figure 8: Eastern Hudson Bay Sea-ice Conditions (circa 1920-1970)

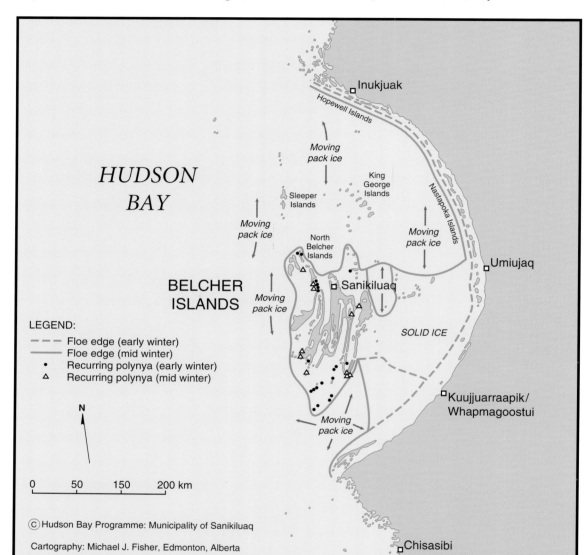

Source: Hudson Bay Programme, *Traditional Ecological Knowledge of Environmental Changes in Hudson and James Bays, Part I.* (Ottawa: HBP, 1995), 36.

Figure 9: Changes in Eastern Hudson Bay Sea-ice Conditions (circa 1970-1993)

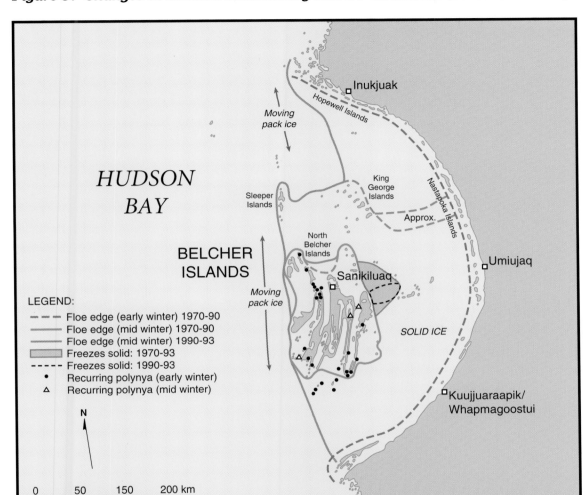

Source: Hudson Bay Programme, *Traditional Ecological Knowledge of Environmental Changes in Hudson and James Bays, Part I.* (Ottawa: HBP, 1995), 37.

Legend for Currents Maps (See pages 35 & 36)

Main Currents. Two main currents were identified in the study: one in Hudson Strait and another that moves water out of southwest Hudson Bay into James Bay. The significance of the Hudson Strait current is that the flow is equally strong in each direction. Community representatives from western James Bay suggest a main current moves water from south-central Hudson Bay into James Bay, where it is channelled by the Twin Islands on the east and Akimiski Island on the west. This idea is supported by Belcher Islands representatives because it explains the open-water area that extends from the southwestern Belcher Islands floe edge during winter months.

Strong Currents. Red arrows indicate strong surface currents that move water in one direction only. They are found either offshore or in the vicinity of river mouths. In addition, three strong currents are situated at the mouth of Hudson Strait between Nottingham Island and the Quebec mainland. The strongest is closest to Nottingham Island, and the least strong is closest to the Quebec mainland. Another strong current on the north side of Hudson Strait moves water from the bay out through the strait.

Tidal Currents keep water and pack ice moving back and forth throughout Hudson Bay during ebb and flood tides. For instance, tidal currents move the pack ice back and forth in Hudson Strait until it is transported out of the system by the strongest current flowing in an easterly direction. The pack ice also moves back and forth with the tides offshore from Wemindji in eastern James Bay.

Weak Currents occur in localized areas of northeastern Hudson Bay except during spring, when there is a lot of melt water and run-off flowing into the bay through the rivers and from the land.

Flood Tide and Ebb Tide indicate the direction of water movement when the tide is coming in (flood tide) and when the tide is going out (ebb tide).

Breaking Points are found either where water from ebb and flood tides meet or where the tides coming in from two different directions meet. Breaking points are generally influenced by local landforms. Some of the breaking points found in Hudson Bay are in Roes Welcome Sound, immediately south of Wager Bay; at the east end of Akimiski Island, just north of Attawapiskat; at the Maquatua River mouth at Wemindji; at Seahorse Point, on Southampton Island; and inside Hudson Strait to the east of Charles Island.

Figure 10: Tidal and Surface Current Activity in Hudson Strait

Source: Hudson Bay Programme, *Traditional Ecological Knowledge of Environmental Changes in Hudson and James Bays, Part II.* (Ottawa: HBP, 1995), 22-i.

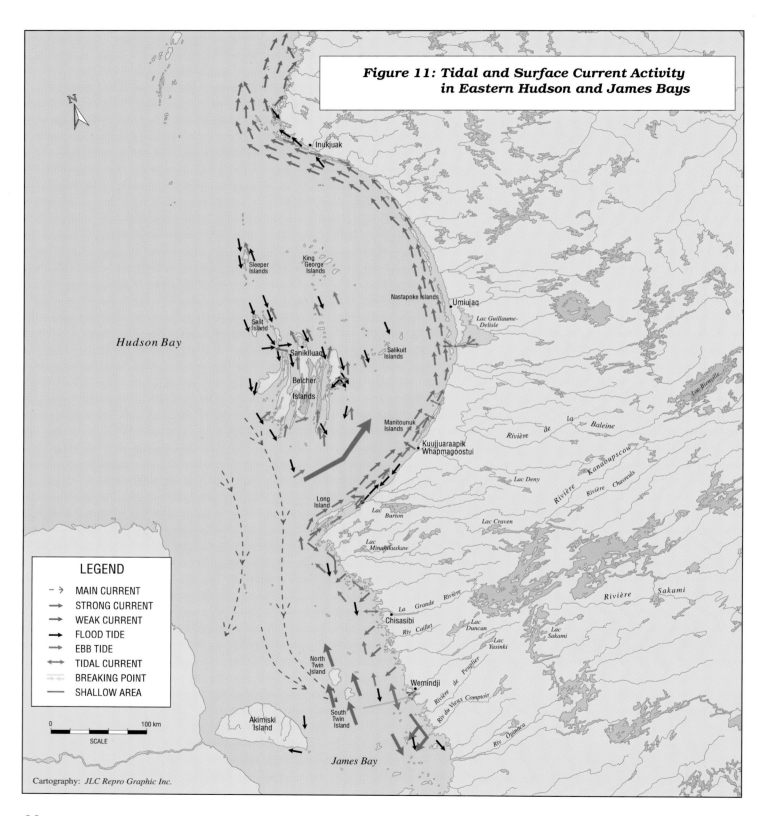

Figure 11: Tidal and Surface Current Activity in Eastern Hudson and James Bays

LEGEND

- - → MAIN CURRENT
- → STRONG CURRENT
- → WEAK CURRENT
- → FLOOD TIDE
- → EBB TIDE
- ↔ TIDAL CURRENT
- BREAKING POINT
- SHALLOW AREA

0   100 km
SCALE

Hudson Bay

Sleeper Islands

King George Islands

Salit Island

Sanikiluaq

Belcher Islands

Nastapoke Islands

Umiujaq

Lac Guillaume-Delisle

Salikuit Islands

Manitounuk Islands

Kuujjuaraapik
Whapmagoostui

Rivière de la Baleine

Lac Bienville

Kanaoupscow

Rivière

Lac Deny

Rivière Chavreulx

Long Island

Lac Burton

Lac Craven

Lac Minahikuskaw

Rivière Sakami

La Grande Rivière

Chisasibi

Riv. Caillet

Lac Duncan

Lac Sakami

Lac Yasinki

North Twin Island

Wemindji

Rivière de Peuplier

South Twin Island

Akimiski Island

Riv. du Vieux Comptoir

Riv. Opinaca

James Bay

Inukjuak

Cartography: *JLC Repro Graphic Inc.*

Salinity

Along the northeastern coast of James Bay, coastal Cree have observed freshwater ice forming farther out in the bay than it used to, dead seals sinking in the Seal and La Grande river estuaries, an increased frequency of diseased mammals in the marine environment, and a growing number of dead sea mammals with no external wounds.[11] They think sea mammals rounding Cape Jones into eastern James Bay are entering water having lower salinity than they need to survive.

Shorelines

Rising land (a natural phenomenon) and both natural and man-made changes in river and near-shore sedimentation are affecting coastal areas and rivers throughout the Hudson Bay bioregion. Rocks are exposed on sandy beaches and shallow areas are now shoals. Shoals are forming new islands near Arviat, York Factory, Peawanuck, Lake River, Moose Factory, Wemindji, and in the Belcher Islands. Manitounuk Sound, which used to have deep water, has become shallow in places—a change that has been noticed since the 1960s. Some northeastern Hudson Bay estuaries are now too shallow for whales to use for moulting. Fish migration in some rivers in Hudson Strait and eastern and northwestern Hudson Bay now depends on adequate rainfall. Grass and trees are growing in tributary creeks and channels of southern James Bay rivers and in rivers altered for hydroelectric power generation.

Shoreline extension and changes in coastal vegetation have significantly modified waterfowl habitat in James Bay and southwestern Hudson Bay over the past 50 years, contributing to the shift in goose flyways. In eastern Hudson Bay, the distance to today's shoreline from *places where our Ancestors used to camp* is greater than gunshot range.

Emerging shorelines are very obvious in James Bay and along the southwestern coast of Hudson Bay where shoals have risen above sea level. The shoreline north of Lake River, for instance, is extending into Hudson Bay and is not shifting in any other direction. Large rocks and sandbars are now visible, and as an island in southwestern Hudson Bay slowly merges with the shoreline fewer walrus are visiting it.

In the York Factory area an old York boat, shipwrecked on a sandbar during the early 1900s, is now approximately 150 metres inland, with all but the ribs buried and covered with white moss and grass. A two-metre boulder, situated about three-quarters of a kilometre offshore during the 1940s, was about 90 metres offshore and submerged only 15 centimetres in 1992.

Since 1955, bank erosion along the Nelson River at Marsh Point and wave action have formed new islands along the shore and fostered vegetation growth where it never existed before. Creeks along Hayes River are forming from underground and have pushed shorelines up approximately two metres.[12] Ice also changes shorelines in the Marsh Point-Gillam Island area when it washes downriver, scraping the river banks in spring.[13]

In southwestern Hudson Bay wind, waves, and currents push ice in to the shoreline with enough force to move boulders. Incoming ice scrapes the underwater sand and mud and piles it along the shore; each time the ice breaks, the muddy sand is carried into the bay, where onshore waves form it into shoreline ridges.

River systems

Rivers throughout the Hudson Bay bioregion are changing as a result of both natural causes and hydroelectric development. In the rivers of northwestern Hudson Bay, weaker currents and lower water levels are altering the migration routes for Arctic char and trout.

On the south side of Hudson Strait, decreasing river levels are attributed to slow melting in spring, less spring and mid-summer rainfall, and the land rising over time. Connecting rivers within the river systems have dried up and qamaniit—places where the widening and deepening of a river assume the dimensions of lakes—no longer exist. In the Ivujivik, Salluit, and Kangiqsujuaq areas the mid-summer river flow is decreasing every year and the connecting lakes have smaller and fewer fish. Shallow water and reduced flow now prevent boats from entering the Kangiqsujuaq River, and the mouth of the Salluit River is too shallow for larger boats to anchor. Lower water levels in rivers on the north side of Hudson Strait are thought to be a result of decreased precipitation.

In eastern Hudson Bay, fish weirs actively used by Elders in their youth now protrude from dry river beds; the rising Hudson Bay landmass and the declining rate of rainfall keep river levels low during summer months. In the Belcher Islands, some creeks have water only during spring run-off or when it rains. Water levels have also decreased in the mouths of Akulivik area rivers and in rivers near Inukjuak, Umiujaq, and Kuujjuaraapik/Whapmagoostui.

Several dams control the Moose, Nelson-Churchill, and La Grande river systems.[14] The flow in La Grande River is increased by the diversion of the Eastmain, Opinaca, and Caniapiscau rivers into it, and the Nelson River flow has been altered by diversion of the Churchill River and regulation of waters in Lake Winnipeg. A number of dams exist on the rivers flowing into the Moose River.

The natural water flow—high in spring/summer and low in fall/winter—has been reversed in these controlled river systems, disrupting normal freezing patterns. In the Nelson River system, for example, water flow begins to rise with higher electrical demand in September and continues to rise throughout the early freezing period. Ice breaks at weak points, and slush builds up and freezes on the shoreline until after the water levels reach maximum height in January or February. During winter, water levels typically rise during the night and fall during the day, causing the ice to shift continually and break up, which creates precarious and unpredictable ice conditions.

In spring, falling water levels leave ice suspended from shorelines, which adversely affects animals and humans' safe use of the shorelines for travelling and hunting:

There is one particular creek that the fish went into in the fall when the water levels were high. In spring, after the water levels went down, the hanging ice dropped and the fish were caught underneath the ice because there was only a little bit of water in the creek.

Donald Saunders, York Landing

River ice conditions in eastern James Bay have changed so much from fluctuating water levels and a modified freezing regime that people have had to alter their travel routes. The ice on some rivers is only about ten centimetres thick in the middle of winter.

Increased winter flow on the lower La Grande prevents solid freezing, and even in the coldest season one cannot freely cross the river at Chisasibi. A community-appointed monitor verifies the safety of the ice and directs pedestrians and snowmobilers onto firm ice. Air pockets under the ice make conditions even more dangerous.[15] Ice quality has deteriorated since the extra powerhouse at LG-2A began operating, and people predicted that it would become even worse when LG-1 (the dam closest to Chisasibi) was completed in 1994.

Since La Grande River was dammed, estuarine and near-shore sea-ice conditions have also changed. The sea ice doesn't freeze as hard, and areas of open water are found in unexpected places. Ice in the offshore current moves at a much faster pace.

Significantly lower water levels have changed shoreline habitat in rivers diverted to the Nelson, Abitibi (southern James Bay), and La Grande rivers. Trees and willows upon which beaver, moose, and ptarmigan feed have dried out and died.

Some rivers, like the Eastmain and Abitibi, do not have water flowing in them any more. In others, water regulation has altered the natural flow and damaged habitat.

The Nelson River used to be a *good, deep, fast river,* but the reduction in summer water levels is so significant that to reach York Factory by canoe travellers now have to connect with water from the incoming tides:

In summer, when the water is released from the dams, it is high as far as Gillam Island which is about nine miles [14.5 kilometres] up the Nelson River from the bay ... the water starts to get low towards Gillam Island, but ... if the tide from Hudson Bay is already flowing into the river ... you can travel all the way down to York Factory. Along the way, there's no drinking water from the main river. You have to get your drinking water from the creeks coming into the river.

Fred Beardy, York Landing

Duck, goose, fish, and moose habitat for about 16 kilometres on the Nelson River upriver from Marsh Point has been severely damaged. Fewer geese and ducks now use what once was an important spring and fall staging area at Marsh Point. Fish that use the small creeks for spawning or travelling to and from the Nelson River get trapped by the fluctuating water levels.

The Moose and Harrikanaw river estuaries are also *very shallow today.* Like the Nelson River, the Moose River is so shallow on one side that boat passage near the mouth of the river is possible only when the tide comes in. People can walk almost from Moosonee to Charles Island at low tide in summer. The Little Abitibi River has dried up since it was diverted into Abitibi River, and the regulation of water flowing through the Abitibi River causes fluctuations in the water levels of the Moose River. Vegetation grows in some channels and water no longer flows in others that Elders (now in their 60s) remember using for canoe travel. In winter, both humans and animals have problems moving across ice left hanging after the water levels go down.

Eastern James Bay Cree have observed deterioration in the taste and quality of fish from the Sakami River since its water level was raised by the diversion of the Eastmain River. Also, when lands were flooded for water impoundment, lake trout, pike, whitefish, brook trout, dore, and sucker intermingled. At first, eastern James Bay Cree found the fish

... very good for eating because what they ate made them more nutritious. But, as we later found out, the fish declined in taste.

William Fireman, Chisasibi

When these lakes are flooded the mixing of water causes the quality to change. I shared my feelings on the consequences, and effects, it would have on the fish ... I said, "The fish would come in contact with things they had never before experienced and that this could cause diseases." Sure enough, it didn't take long for the good quality fish to decline, and fish were known to contain high levels of mercury.

John Matches, Wemindji

Since rivers entering Hudson and James bays have been dammed for hydroelectric generation, increased volumes of sediment and debris have directly affected aboriginal fisheries:[16]

In their publications, [Hydro-Québec] wrote there was no change in where we got our fish since their projects [began]. In a meeting, I informed them that, for three years now, I could not even lift my net when I checked it because it was so heavy with river debris. They had no comments on what I told them.

This is where we used to set our nets in summer. Now, we cannot do that because all the river debris reaches this area ... when you put your net on this side of the island it is full of debris that comes from the river. You cannot get as much fish as you used to. This river running here had a lot of fish long ago just as this other river did. In fall, you could always get a lot of fish here. At LG-1, in the summer, you could scoop a lot of fish from the rapids before they put up a dam.

Jimmy Rupert, Chisasibi

In the Nelson River, sediment accumulation covers the food of bottom-feeders:

The river flow increases when the water is released [by Manitoba Hydro] so you get all that debris from the river bottom. Then, the water levels go down and it gets muddy as the sediment settles. Then, when the water is not moving, the slime builds up.

York Factory Cree

And pollutants are a concern:

The Churchill River has been diverted into the Nelson River so it's now picking up pollutants from Thompson and the Inco mine. You can see that the

water is polluted and can destroy where it is shallow. There is green slime on the bottom which goes from the river into the creeks. It used to be clear where I trap but when I was chopping a hole in the ice, in spring, you could see the water was polluted.

York Factory Cree

La Grande River once provided *the purest* drinking water, but now area residents drink neither from La Grande nor from the Eastmain or Nelson rivers.[17] Cree and Inuit living outside the eastern James Bay area find it shocking that people of Eastmain now rely on bottled drinking water.

Fish and wildlife

Inuit and Cree are directly affected when animal, fish, and bird populations change in the Hudson Bay region. As a result of both naturally occurring and human-induced changes, wildlife habitat is disappearing.

The rising landmass is impeding river access for anadromous fish and seal populations in Arctic coastal areas. Naturally occurring shoreline extensions are causing structural changes to waterfowl habitat in sub-Arctic coastal areas.

In the Nelson, Moose, and La Grande river systems, habitat has been reduced for more than 15 species of animals, birds, and fish. Many of the creeks and small rivers in the Nelson River system that once supported wild rice have been flooded, and consequently the duck population has declined. Beaver, muskrat, ptarmigan, grouse, rabbit, and moose populations have also responded to irrecoverable loss of food resources from river diversions, damming, logging, and mining.

Sturgeon, whitefish, lake trout, and dore are some of the fish species losing critical river spawning sites in eastern James Bay, western Hudson Bay, and southern James Bay.[18]

A decline in local walrus numbers observed by James Bay and southwestern Hudson Bay Cree is associated with changing shorelines and habitat alteration. Walrus used to inhabit Cape Hope Island, but the depressions they made in the ground are now

41

overgrown with willow. Lots of walrus also inhabited an island in the Winisk area until it began merging with the coastal shoreline in the early 1980s. Now they return only to visit, in groups of two or three.

Animal populations in any given locality in the Hudson Bay region may change in different ways: natural fluctuations may occur; populations may shift locations in response to habitat loss, food availability, or other disturbances; reproduction rates can fluctuate in response to food availability or unseasonable weather; disturbed habitat may cause deteriorating health and body condition; and human interference in natural processes can initiate population response:[19]

Let me use caribou and walrus as examples. Our Elders say that any kind of animal moves away for awhile but, according to the government, animals are in decline. To the Inuit, they have moved, but not declined. We were told that before we were born caribou were on the mainland, but they moved to another area. Our Elders said, "they'll come back again." It was the same thing with walrus. From what I have heard, there used to be lots of walrus here. Now there isn't, but they're not gone. They have just moved. Also, in our community, there is a place called Ullikuluk where there hardly used to be any walrus. Now, there are many. The government says they become extinct when really they have just moved.

Peter Alogut, Coral Harbour

Rabbit, caribou, lemming, and fox naturally experience wide population fluctuations. Both Inuit and Cree in northern Quebec suggest caribou are now peaking in their cycle and may experience a sharp drop in numbers in coming years. They note several indicators, including high population numbers, caribou moving into areas they don't normally inhabit, a greater reliance on secondary food resources, increased incidence of liver disease, and deterioration of body conditions.

In western Hudson Bay, *the beginning of the end of lynx* coincided with the establishment of radar sites, and sightings over the past 10 to 15 years have been very rare. Recently, however, lynx have started appearing north of Churchill in the Arviat area. Similarly, moose, in response to habitat loss and disturbance in eastern James Bay, are moving into the Kuuj-juaraapik/Whapmagoostui area.

Canada and snow goose migrations have shifted east, from the Quebec coast towards the mountains of mid-northern Quebec. Along the Manitoba and northwestern Ontario coasts, more geese are entering and leaving Hudson Bay from the west and fewer are taking the north-south coastal route. Cree attribute this significant change to a combination of effects over the last 20 years: weather system changes; coastal and inland habitat changes; disturbance from inexperienced hunters who haven't learnt how to hunt and treat geese properly; and wildlife management interference—including use of aircraft, handling of eggs for nesting surveys, and leg and collar banding for population studies—at critical times in the goose reproductive cycle.[20]

Because marine mammals respond to environmental conditions by always moving in search of food, a population decline in one area may signal not an overall decrease in numbers but rather a shift to an area where conditions are more favourable. Fewer beluga are now seen in James Bay and along the eastern coast of Hudson Bay; more are seen in the offshore areas of eastern Hudson Bay. Fewer whales now visit the mouths of the Churchill and Nelson rivers; large numbers are reported in the vicinity of the Winisk and Severn rivers, where whitefish are abundant.

Inuit in eastern and northwestern Hudson Bay report increasing numbers of polar bears, and Cree in southwestern Hudson Bay have observed female polar bears with more than two cubs. Eastern Hudson Bay Inuit, who have seen the numbers increase since the 1930s—and more rapidly since the 1960s—think the polar bears are relocating to eastern Hudson Bay in response to the effects of an abundance of ringed seals, the extended floe edge, and hunting quotas in effect since the 1970s.

Both Inuit and Cree know that, without traditional hunting and trapping, the population of many marine and terrestrial animals decreases over time. Although local populations often initially increase in response to reduced hunting and trapping, the animals eventually diminish their food supply and either move to a new area or die from starvation—conditions that reduce rates of reproduction. Snowy owls, for example, don't breed when the lemming population is low but begin breeding again as it increases. Walrus and beaver respond similarly when they diminish their food supply:

The prohibition was for a long time, and the beaver multiplied and were dying before the game wardens allowed trapping to start again. Married men with families were allowed ten, and single men got five, when they finally opened up the season. I don't know how many years this went on but, when the beaver started to die, there was so many that they said we could take as many as we could. I went down a creek the year before the Ministry of Natural Resources released that policy. The following year somebody else went down the same creek, and saw dead beaver lying on the shore one right after another. It was too late. The beaver already died from overpopulation because they weren't harvested. They had no more food, and killed the areas where they were. It seems the beaver population increases when no one is harvesting, which leads them to outstrip their food supply and destroy creeks. The numbers start to go down from disease and death.

Fred Beardy, York Landing

Natural indicators for animal health are seasonal fat thickness, liver condition, meat colour, fur condition, and behaviour. Inuit and Cree also notice a difference in the taste and behaviour of animals that feed in contaminated areas or on human-generated waste.

Contamination has affected areas used by geese, ducks, and fish to feed. Malnourished fish have been found in water systems contaminated from mining activity in northern Quebec. Body changes are occurring in sturgeon affected by hydro activities in the La Grande, Nottaway, and Moose river systems.

Fox, sea gulls, crows, and ravens are no longer part of the Inuit diet because they are known to *eat anything* and today that includes human garbage. Polar bear, jaegers, falcons, and snowy owls are natural hunters, but they are also scavengers when hungry. Western Hudson Bay Cree have learnt that polar bears foraging hunting camps consume motor oil. Northwestern Hudson Bay Inuit have seen how oil blackens the polar bears' stomach contents and emits an offensive odour when in the stomach too long. They have also seen caribou and geese feeding in sewage lagoons. Eastern James Bay Cree report that black bears have lost their sense of territoriality since they started feeding at work camp and community garbage sites.

Impact of environmental change

Because traditional Cree and Inuit remain heavily dependent on locally available natural foods, they are sensitive to how contaminants affect the Hudson Bay ecosystem and damage humans and animals. They also are afraid that as more and more of their natural foods are damaged by hydroelectric development, logging, mining, and contaminants, their traditions and ways of life have less chance of surviving.

Cree report many changes occurring in animal populations since hydroelectric development and logging altered the natural environment in their respective areas:

> *Travelling to my territory, inland from LG-2, I see that the trees are dying on both sides of the rivers. It is happening all over the inland flooded areas. The destruction is already spreading 200 feet [60 metres] from the shoreline. The sturgeon, along with other species of fish, are also affected. They are on the decline, more so than at the beginning of the flooding. There were plenty of fish before all this happened. Now it is a different story. There are less fish in the lakes on the hunting territories. It is the same with the birds, especially the willow ptarmigan. During winter there used to be plenty of them.... The impact on the people from these changes has been great.... There have been too many changes....*

William Fireman, Chisasibi

> *We were still able to harvest a good number of animals and fish when the reservoirs were first created. Now it's as if everything is gone. There are only two lakes, where we used to fish, that haven't been flooded over. I am talking about lakes where fish were healthy and plentiful. In spring, we used to camp at the mouth of a river. There were two tributaries on this river, and the ice would go from this area at a fast pace. We trapped*

> *for otter, muskrat, and beavers. Now this river is gone. It is completely flooded over. I have not been able to catch any beaver from there for the last three years because they have disappeared.*

John Matches, Wemindji

Beaver, otter, muskrat, and fish are particularly affected by the change in water flow regimes, and moose, geese, ptarmigan, and rabbit populations are responding to habitat loss; as a result, the diets of both coastal and inland Cree have been directly affected.

Figure 12 summarizes environmental changes observed by Inuit and Cree in the six traditional land-use and occupancy areas in the Hudson Bay region.

Detailed information on sturgeon, snow geese, Canada geese, beluga whale, and polar bear is found in appendices D and E.

Notes

1. The western Hudson Bay region includes the land-use and occupancy areas of the Fort Severn, Shamattawa, and York Factory Cree nations. Its coastal area extends from Churchill to south of Fort Severn. The York Factory Indian Band now resides in York Landing and, although remote from their traditional lands in the York Factory area, people continue to use the coastal area.

2. The western James Bay region includes the land-use and occupancy area of the Peawanuck, Attawapiskat, Kashechewan, Fort Albany, and Moose Factory Cree. Its coastal area, therefore, extends from north of Peawanuck in southwestern Hudson Bay to the Ontario-Quebec border in southern James Bay.

3. The eastern James Bay coastal area extends from the Ontario-Quebec border to Cape Jones at the southeast corner of Hudson Bay. The area is inhabited mainly by Cree, although some Inuit continue to live in Chisasibi. Most Inuit living on the offshore islands of eastern James Bay were relocated to Great Whale River in 1960.

4. The eastern Hudson Bay coastal area extends from Cape Jones to Cape Smith Island just north of Akulivik. Kuujjuaraapik Inuit hunt and camp in coastal areas extending to Long Island at Cape Jones. Whapmagoostui Cree hunt and trap in lands and rivers extending up to Richmond Gulf. The Belcher Islands are also part of the eastern Hudson Bay area.

5. The Hudson Strait region includes the land-use and occupancy areas of Baffin Island Inuit from Cape Dorset and Lake Harbour and Nunavik Inuit from Ivujivik, Salluit, and Kangiqsujuaq. It also includes Nottingham, Mansel, and Salisbury islands.

6. A similar process is happening in the Nottaway-Rupert-Broadback river system from metal waste at industrial sites. Ice pushes scrap metal into rivers during spring break-up, where it corrodes, causing oil and gas to leak, in some cases, into the

water system, affecting both the appearance and the taste of fish. Oil and gas have also leaked into the system at abandoned defence installations and along the winter roads in western Hudson Bay, affecting geese.

7. Western Hudson Bay and eastern James Bay representatives identified bears, geese, and fish as other species whose eating habits and behaviour are being directly affected by the growing amount of garbage and oil and gas spillage.

8. This observation was reported by community representatives in eastern Hudson Bay, Hudson Strait, northwestern Hudson Bay, western Hudson Bay, southwestern Hudson Bay, and western James Bay. Some recent haze effects may have been related to the global effects of the 1991 eruption of Mount Pinatubo.

9. Freezing snow in June 1992 affected the geese nesting in the Arviat area as well as in western and southwestern Hudson Bay.

10. Post-glacial uplift continues at a rate of a few feet [one foot = approximately 30 centimetres] each century in many parts of Hudson Bay.

11. Seals usually float when they die during the fall months.

12. This figure is from a scientific study reported to the community.

13. On large sections of the Nelson River ice scouring erodes mud, soil, trees, and other sediment, forming shoals. In recent years the size of mud slides has increased in areas where gravel and earth become saturated with water and no longer have the strength to prevent river banks from collapsing.

14. These three rivers drain much of southern Alberta and Saskatchewan and most of Manitoba, northern Ontario, and northeastern Quebec.

15. Air pockets as much as two and one-half metres above water level and areas of weak ice make travel on the Nelson River hazardous as well.

16. The nets become very heavy with mud, debris, and slime and yield few fish.

17. Hudson Bay TEKMS Workshop I. Sanikiluaq: October 1992.

18. Cree traditional knowledge of sturgeon's sensitivity to water change and disturbance may qualify it as a key water-quality indicator species.

19. Traditional Cree and Inuit have difficulty accepting wildlife management decisions that target their hunting or trapping practices without examining all the environmental factors influencing a population.

20. Inland habitat changes include creation of both reservoirs in eastern Quebec and waterfowl habitat on the prairies.

Figure 12: Regional Environmental Changes Observed by Inuit and Cree

	Eastern James Bay	Eastern Hudson Bay	Hudson Strait	Northwestern Hudson Bay	Western Hudson Bay	Western James Bay
Weather	• shorter spring & fall seasons • greater variability in fall • colder winters in reservoir areas • increased snowfall	• persistence of cold weather into spring • snow melts later • spring and summer cooling trend • less rain; fewer thunderstorms	• greater variability; less predictable • cooling trend • new snowfall cycle • longer winters; snow melts later • less rainfall	• greater variability • warmer and shorter winters • snow falls and melts earlier • cool summers in early 1990s	• longer winters • colder springs • snow melts faster	• shorter and warmer winters • spring wind shifts several times a day
Atmosphere	• change in sky colour	• change in sky colour • sun's heat blocked by haze	• change in sky colour • sun's heat blocked by haze	• change in sky colour	• change in sky colour	• change in sky colour
Sea ice	• salinity changing along north-east coast • more freshwater ice forming in the bay • less solid in La Grande River area; freezes later, breaks earlier	• freezes faster • solid ice cover is larger and thicker • fewer polynyas • floe edge melts before breaking up	• freezes faster • poorer quality • landfast ice extends farther offshore • polynyas freeze • floe edge melts before breaking up			
Currents	• weaker in Eastmain area • swifter and less predictable north of La Grande River	• weakening currents	• weakening currents	• weaker currents in Roes Welcome Sound		
Rivers	• seasonal reversal in levels and flow • decline in water quality • unstable ice conditions on La Grande River; freezes later, breaks earlier • vegetation dying along diverted rivers	• decreased water levels and river flow	• decreased water levels and river flow	• decreased water levels and river flow	• seasonal reversal in water levels and flow • increased salinity, erosion and sediment in Nelson River • decline in water quality	• decreased water levels and river flow in southern James Bay rivers • increased erosion and mud slides
Canada and snow geese	• coastal and inland habitat changes • coastal flyways have shifted eastward • fewer being harvested in spring and fall • large flocks of non-nesting/ moulting geese along coastal flyway	• smaller flocks of Canada geese arrive in Belcher Islands since 1984 • increase in non-nesting/ moulting geese in Belcher and Long islands	• new snow goose migration routes • increase in number of moulting snow geese • Canada geese no longer nest in Soper River area	• more Canada geese in Repulse Bay area during summers of 1992 and 1993	• more snow geese migrating to and from the west • habitat changes at Marsh Point staging area • earlier and shorter fall migration	• habitat changes in Moose Factory area • more snow geese flying in from the west • Canada geese arrive from the north first part of June • change in fall migration patterns

	Eastern James Bay	Eastern Hudson Bay	Hudson Strait	Northwestern Hudson Bay	Western Hudson Bay	Western James Bay
Beluga whale	• decrease in numbers	• decrease in numbers along coast • moved to and travelling in currents farther offshore	• decrease in numbers in Salluit area	• decrease in numbers in Repulse Bay and Arviat area	• increase in numbers in Fort Severn and Winisk estuaries • decrease in numbers in Nelson River estuary	
Fish	• mercury contamination • loss of adequate habitat for several species, e.g., whitefish, sturgeon, pike • morphological changes in sturgeon	• decrease in Arctic char and Arctic cod in Inukjuak area		• decrease in Arctic cod in near-shore areas • Arctic cod no longer found in near-shore areas off Cape Smith and Repulse Bay	• mercury contamination • loss of habitat including spawning grounds • change in taste of fish; some are inedible	• morphological changes in sturgeon • dried river channels
Polar bear		• increase in numbers since 1960s	• decrease in numbers in Ivujivik area	• increase in numbers • appear leaner and more aggressive	• thin-looking bears in York Factory area • drink motor oil • change in behaviour	• recent increase in reproduction rates • fearless of humans
Walrus	• no longer present in Wemindji area	• shift away from Belcher Islands	• increase in numbers around Nottingham Island	• decrease in numbers near Arviat and Whale Cove • increase in numbers near Coral Harbour and Chesterfield Inlet		• decrease in numbers in Attawapiskat area
Moose	• loss of habitat • decrease in numbers • change in body condition • change in taste of meat	• in-migration from southeastern James Bay			• change in taste of meat • greater number drowning • no moose at Marsh Point	
Caribou	• change in body condition and behaviour • increase in number of diseased livers and intestines • change in diet • change in taste of meat • more caribou along the coast	• caribou from different areas mingle together • very large herds • travelling closer to coast • change in diet • change in taste of meat	• increase in numbers • increase in abnormal livers, e.g., spots and lumps • change in diet	• increase in numbers • not intimidated by exploration activity • feed close to exploration camps • change in diet	• increase in numbers • Pin Island herd is mixing with Woodland herd	

"When the system is healthy you are healthy.
When the system is polluted it kills you slowly."

Indigenous Perspectives on Development

In a very real sense, the cultural, economic, and physical health of indigenous people in the Hudson Bay bioregion reflects the health of their natural environment—an environment subject to change from both natural forces and human activities. While many Cree and Inuit deplore the environmental changes they observe and wonder how they will pass on their ecological knowledge and time-proven values to coming generations, they know that change will continue. Their realism in the face of powerful outside forces is tempered by their determination to sustain their culture and economy and to care for the environment upon which both are based.

Industrial development in the north began with the arrival of the first European explorers, missionaries, and fur traders and continued as seasonal communities were transformed into permanent settlements with new administrative, political, and economic infrastructure and later with modern education and health services. During the last few decades, mining, logging, and large-scale hydroelectric projects have been developed—in most cases, with little attention to the human ecological impacts:

I could have brought a lot of paper on all the measurements of the different impacts that they now know. That material is available and there's no problem if somebody wants to get it because it's all on paper. But, what we never really hear about is the human impact. The impact on humans and impact on communities. All the studies are very specialized in studying the effects of development on certain physical things in the environment. There is really no complete picture of what it does to our people, the community, animals, and the whole environment.

Helen Atkinson, Chisasibi

... people living inside the Hudson and James Bay basin have experienced major effects from forestry, mining, and hydroelectric developments because the hunting areas and animal habitats have been damaged. The hunting way of life has been affected by those developments and ...

people have had to stop relying on wildlife. In Chisasibi, people had to stop fishing in their surrounding areas. In Eastmain, they now buy water for drinking ... relocation has changed and affected their way of life.

Lucassie Arragutainaq, Sanikiluaq

Industrial development will continue to affect the Hudson Bay bioregion, its peoples, and its resources; thus it is important to gain an appreciation of indigenous peoples' views of industrial development and of the impact it has on their traditional way of life:

So, what the development has done is to make hunting territories smaller by flooding a lot of land, and opening up the territory to sport hunters. The environment is damaged. The animals are sick. The animals are changing their patterns. That's bad in and of itself, but when they don't understand our lifestyle, and that we need our way of life, it's a slap in the face.

Helen Atkinson, Chisasibi

Socio-cultural considerations

One of the things development totally ignores about the land is the native burial grounds. The burial grounds were actually like the holy land to us long ago. It's very natural for our people to respect these areas.

Louis Bird, Peawanuck

In 1941, when I was a little boy, a tradition existed among our people. People used the bush as home base. During hunting, in wintertime, families left the community. Only a few stayed behind. When the radar base was established, there was an opportunity for our trappers to earn a living for a 10-year period. That's when our tradition began to disappear because men had to work at the base and the women had to stay in the community. So, their lifestyle was changing. Their food was also changing ... [and] the body system of the men was

49

changing. Over the 10-year period, men were able to digest the white man's food. ...They began to imitate the way the white people dressed. Our men used to wear clothing that was suitable for hunting in the bush. Now, they were wearing suits, ties, and shiny shoes. The men were now almost totally alienated from their tradition. Ever since the Europeans came to this bay, our tradition has been changing but it changed in a big way over a period of 10 or 15 years.

Louis Bird, Peawanuck

In 1964, we first encountered the white man coming from the south. The plane landed in Great Whale and they took another aircraft inland. The Cree people were not informed why these people came up there. They went inland with all their equipment including canoes. They put markings on the trees. When I saw this, I asked about the markings on the trees. I was told that all the rivers in Quebec would be dammed. We did not know what to do next. I was on the Band Council at that time, and we thought we should at least get some compensation so we made the agreement with Hydro-Québec and the governments. It is still the case, today, that they have not lived up to the agreement.

Joseph Petagumskum, Whapmagoostui

Relocation, schools, and health services

The federal relocation policy centralized administrative, housing, education, health, and welfare services and the federal government proceeded to relocate Cree and Inuit living in seasonal camps to the present settlements. For example, when the coastal community of York Factory was closed in 1957, Cree were relocated inland to York Landing. Inuit living on the James Bay islands were relocated to Great Whale River in 1960 and Inuit living in the south Belcher Islands were moved to the north Belcher Islands when the federal government established the community of Sanikiluaq in 1970. The Cree and Inuit living in Fort George were relocated to the new community of Chisasibi under the James Bay and Northern Quebec Agreement.

In the old days, the people used to travel widely up and down the coast and use inland rivers as needed. Now that they're living here in York Landing they hardly ever get to go anywhere. There's no resources to live off either. Our area is completely surrounded by Split Lake trappers. The young people can't go anywhere so they stay here. There's no survival activities like hunting, fishing, and trapping because the resources belong to the

Split Lake people. We've been sent to a poor area here, and have nothing. It's just like being wedged between two rocks with no place to go. The young people like to go out, but it's such a small area. I've seen young people who like to go hunting. It shows in the spring time. They also like to trap around here but, further than that, you cannot go any place. They show a lot of interest in the traditional way of life but there's no resources.

York Factory Cree

As a result of relocating our people to where we're presently living, we've lost our culture, especially the young people. We lost our resources, and our traditional areas for meeting and acquiring traditional knowledge. Today, we are losing our language.

Donald Saunders, York Landing

As far back as the 1940s and 50s, the federal government had a policy that said if we did not send our children to school we would be punished and even put in jail. That's how strongly the government insisted we put the children in school. It is a very powerful imposition having a different culture imposed upon you because when our children went to school they lost the importance of hunting which is why we have lost the old traditional way of our culture. Education, itself, has slowly destroyed our culture.

Gabriel Fireman, Attawapiskat

I keep thinking that our people have not been looked after in terms of health for well over the past ten years. Our regional health service seems to have forgotten about our bodies. They have focused mostly on animals, and our environment, but have left the humans behind. Maybe because human beings have no dollar value, but animals and our environment can make profits and create jobs so they have lots of dollar value. Medical services used to give us medication, or shots, for measles and other things. We used to get medications every year for all those things. We were even weighed. Nowadays ... the only time they are interested in us is when they find out we are sick.

Also, for some reason, those people diagnosed [with] cancer and the people who have lost their nervous systems appear in large numbers now. In the past, it wasn't like that. The problem could be our diets as a result of eating so much store-bought foods, or something we don't know about. ... more and more people are getting sick. [Also], the medical people are not explaining the reasons and they don't seem to try to find out why it is happening. If we were to know the reasons we would try to help in any way we could. At the same time, we would try to keep ourselves healthy.

Johnny Epoo, Inukjuak

Mixed economy

In the 1990s the Cree and Inuit live with a mixed economy consisting of traditional land-based, wage labour, and market sectors. These three sectors are linked within each community economy and often compete for land and resources. For example, mining, logging, and hydro activities occur in traditional hunting and trapping territories that provide the basis of the Cree economic system, thereby restricting traditional economic opportunities. Aboriginal peoples are severely challenged in adjusting to a mixed economy:

There's no way that the dollar will replace the very delicate environment of ours.

Simon Makimmak, Akulivik

It is impossible not to want or need money now. People often say we must not think of money, but it is impossible to do without it completely. We have to make a living.

John Matches, Wemindji

We now sell meat which we didn't in the past. We were encouraged by our Elders to share our food and it's not the same anymore. It has evolved ... but it's not the Inuit way. It came from the white people as a way to make money. It would be very sad if I was to sell meat to my brothers because it is not my way as an Inuk. I don't have anything against people selling meat to earn some money, but I'm not satisfied with the fact of selling meat to other Inuit.

Peter Alogut, Coral Harbour

We, as hunters, have no other way of earning money [than to use some animals].

Lucassie Iqaluk, Inukjuak

51

Developers are looking at the dollar sign and nothing else. They don't care about the environment or the people who will be directly affected by the dams. All they are looking at is how much they will earn in profits. That's the white man's way of doing things. Some of our leaders are also only looking at how to get the money. They don't seem to really care about our future, or our environments.

Quitsak Tarkiasuk, Ivujivik

Even though we, as Inuit, say, "No, we don't approve of such a thing," they never listen to us. They go ahead and do what they want because it means money. We know it means we will have to stop hunting animals in the coming years if we don't do anything about it.

Lucassie Arragutainaq, Sanikiluaq

Rivers, lakes, and forests contribute a lot to the well-being of a people. These locations were taken over by the white man, who has made a lot of money from them.

George Diamond, Sr., Waskaganish

We virtually have no river anymore. There's a whole series of dams right near the headwaters, and we live with the impact of development full force. There is no buffer at all. The first dam on the river is 30 kilometres from our town, so it's right in our backyard.

Helen Atkinson, Chisasibi

The land has been altered so much in these past 20 years. When they start on [the Great Whale hydroelectric complex] the work is supposed to last 10 years or more. This work will supposedly bring a better standard of life.

Joseph Petagumskum, Whapmagoostui

Hydroelectric development

In the same way that sea ice and currents are revered and valued by Inuit, rivers and creeks are sacred and central to Cree well-being. A Cree Elder reminds us:

It is very important to know how the river functions. When we bother the river we destroy it and divert the ecosystem. It is contrary to how we were

told to use the river. When we dam the system, the fish are destroyed. They are no good. They are inedible. They swim far into the muskeg. They become poisoned and tainted with pollutants. Other living things in this ecosystem are affected and destroyed by damming rivers. We should not allow the river system to be changed.

Fred Beardy, York Landing

The combined effect of river diversions, reversed water flow, and fluctuating water levels from hydroelectric development in the Nelson, La Grande, and Moose river systems has had major impacts on traditional Cree livelihoods.

La Grande River system

I think it's fair to say that we feel invaded. We have been invaded because, first, there is the hydro development and, second, it has opened the door for sport hunters because of the different land categories the Government of Quebec has made. They say, "okay, in this category you can live, this category only you can hunt, and this category anybody can hunt." They don't even consider that land is somebody's traditional hunting territory that was passed onto him to care for and which he wants to pass onto his sons to care for.

Helen Atkinson, Chisasibi

Every year, I go back to my hunting territory and witness effects that the hydroelectric project had in the past year. There's been a lot of land and environment destroyed. At least nine or ten hunting territories are flooded.

Robbie Matthews, Chisasibi

Nelson River system

The water levels are continuously fluctuating. Before the dams, they were high in spring and summer, low in fall and winter. Since the dams, water levels are low in spring and summer, high in fall and winter. In the fall, the animals need lower water but people in the south need electricity so water levels are pretty high.

York Factory Cree

When water is released from the dam, the tide coming in from the bay pushes it back, and it covers the grassland. At Marsh Point, it backs up to where the grass and trees are growing inland. [It] destroys the area there because [salt water] gets into the grass and doesn't go back out with the tide. We went to the places where we used to catch fish. We didn't get any fish. I stopped in four places along the river including this beautiful spot where there used to be fish, but there was none. The creeks were low right then. The water has damaged the wildlife. It was beautiful where we used to hunt at Marsh Point. Now, water floods the land and ice tears the land and trees. It never freezes solid. The ice keeps breaking. It looks like spring break-up with piles of ice on shorelines. Grass, brush, trees are destroyed. It's crushed by ice. Mud piles up on the island when spring break-up comes. There are not really any geese or ducks there anymore.

Fred Beardy, York Landing

Moose River system

When we first heard that Ontario Hydro had plans to build six new dams on the Moose River system in 1989 we started saying there are enough dams on the river now. It's badly damaged enough, and it shouldn't be damaged anymore.

John Turner, Moose Factory

Great Whale River system

... the animals will be affected and our hunting will be altered. There are plenty of caribou in our area right now, but when the activity starts it will be different because all that work will be occurring where the caribou winter every year. All the animals that inhabit the forest will be affected when it is flooded.

Joseph Petagumskum, Whapmagoostui

Once they finish the Kuujjuaraapik hydro project, they will start working on damming our river system where we fish and hunt. All of the larger lakes will be diked, and made into one huge lake in order to make one big river for electric power stations. It's scary when you think about our animals, culture, and hunting way of life.

Charlie Arngak, Kangiqsujuaq

Grand Canal project

In the fall of 1990 or 91, I saw a helicopter on the Harrikanaw River. It was flying from upstream and going in a zigzag on the left-hand side. Then, it went all the way out to the river mouth. There was a guy trapping at the river mouth and he saw the helicopter come up again on the other side of the river. The following summer, I saw ribbons tied on the shore and in the bush. I've wondered if maybe the reason they did all that testing on the river was because they're thinking of diking Hudson Bay and converting the water in James Bay to freshwater to sell to the Americans. They might be thinking of using the Harrikanaw River for that. I heard it will be done by another 20 or 30 years.

Jimmy Small, Moose Factory

Mining

The worst part of the mining pollution is the salt-like chemical they use for thawing or melting snow and ice. They use it to keep their drinking water hole open through the winter in the camps. They just throw it onto the ice, and it keeps the ice open. Some of the fish in that lake do not look good at all.

Amaamak Jaaka, Kangiqsujuaq

Near Cochrane, where one person from our Band traps, they have cut all the trees down, and there's a gold mine there now. Also, some of the lakes are dead now from the mine tailings. He says everything has changed, the fish and even the ducks. The people doing the damage are not even aware that it is a trapping area, and it doesn't look like a trapline anymore either. Roads have been built and all kinds of trucks come there now.

Emma Echum, Moose Factory

Forestry

The hydro dams on the Nelson River are not the only industry in northwestern Manitoba; a single large forestry development covers 108,000 square kilometres of Manitoba—20% of the province and 73% of its trees.[1]

Logging activity is also encroaching upon traditional territories in both the Moose and Nottaway-Rupert river systems:

In our hunting territory, the lumber companies are very close to our trapline. They have already cut trees on the trapline next to ours, and they will probably be cutting trees on our trapline as well.

54

Even though it is a good area for moose, there is already a change in the number of moose. I have noticed a decline in the moose population since they have started cutting near our trapline. The moose have started moving to another area. It did this before, and it is moving further and further away from our area.

George Diamond, Sr., Waskaganish

Forest fire management

Although most forest fires in Cree hunting and trapping territories occur as a result of lightning strikes, allowing them to run a natural course is not consistent with the land-use and lifestyle changes the Cree have had to make in the past 40-50 years. Resettlement policies and other government-imposed land-use restrictions have required the Cree in western James Bay and western Hudson Bay to adapt to fixed territories with limited resources. Subsequently, they no longer have the opportunity to relocate in response to fire-induced changes to the habitat supporting their traditional activities.

In Manitoba and Ontario, provincial policy allows uncontrolled burning of forest fires beyond 16 kilometres from a community. For the Cree in western Hudson Bay, this is a disturbing policy:

Twice we have had meetings with the Ministry of Natural Resources about allowing fires to burn uncontrolled. We told them the ashes and charcoal travelling in the area end up in lakes, rivers, small creeks, and spawning areas where the fish are. Fish is one of our major sources of food, and the food isn't the same when ashes fall into the water and settle on the bottom. The fish caught in the lake after a fire are of very poor quality, and not good for eating. They are soft, and you can still taste the fire. They also swim away from the shallow areas when there's a fire. Other animals try to get away from the fire too. Moose leave those burnt areas, and it's a good three years before they come back. The marten and beaver still haven't returned to their areas since the 1989 forest fire. We told them to consider that whenever a fire occurs in northwestern Ontario, it takes 50 to 70 years before the forest comes back. It's slower than down south because of the weather and heat. Also, the same trees will not grow back. Pine trees grow in burnt areas.

I have heard, but don't agree with, their reasons to allow fires to burn uncontrolled because they don't know how far the natives use the land. A native person covers a number of square miles when he goes out on the land. It's not like he stays on the highway and does not go off the road. Another reason I don't agree is because many people become ill when there are big fires. There was a lot of fires in northwest Ontario and Manitoba during 1989 and 1990. The smoke was so dense, even when the fire was at a fair distance, that many people in the communities had asthma attacks. In the meetings, they said it cost too much to put forest fires out.

Stanley Thomas, Fort Severn

Shipping and offshore exploration

We no longer hear of people disliking ships coming into our community, but we know the sounds they make are affecting animals because the belugas don't come in anymore.

John Kaunak, Repulse Bay

The whales come a little later in the season now because of the shipping traffic. We can see the whales are a little further out of the river mouth than the ships, and they seem to move somewhere else for moulting since the ships are larger than they are.

Sappa Fleming, Kuujjuaraapik

There are no belugas near our community when the ships are there. No sea mammals are there when the ships are. We don't like the ships being there when the belugas are around. We used to think that belugas were attracted by ship movements. Actually, they were trying to get away from the ships.

Jack Angoo, Whale Cove

Today, there's noise all along the shorelines but there was not so much noise before. The ships passing through Hudson Strait used to move the animals to the shorelines. Now, the ships don't seem to have any effects on animals because there is so much noise all around the Hudson Strait.

Peter Audlaluk, Ivujivik

Sea mammals would try to avoid contact with oil exploration activity because of their sensitive

hearing. Another problem with oil explorations is that crude oil is transported by supertankers. If there is ever a mishap while they are transporting the oil, and a large amount of oil was spilled, it would have major repercussions on the whole region.

John Kaunak, Repulse Bay

In the 1970s, the seals' hides were full of oil because the ships used to dump engine oil into the sea. They would dump engine oil in the Repulse Bay harbour when the ships were anchored. The shore would be black with oil slick when there was a south wind. Although we heard this kind of incident occurred in Coral Harbour last year, it is not the case now in Repulse Bay. Perhaps they do their dumping after leaving the communities.

John Kaunak, Repulse Bay

Contaminants and pollutants

It appears that all rivers in the Hudson Bay watershed, including those from United States, flow to our bay: through streams that enter into larger rivers that enter into the bay. When you think about it, Hudson and James bays are like sewage lagoons for every piece of garbage being dumped by southerners into their rivers.

Lucassie Arragutainaq, Sanikiluaq

Contaminants have a variety of sources for getting into the food chain. One source is pollution in the atmosphere. Another source is contaminants coming from the ground. Another source is through the river systems and the fish in those rivers.

Donat Milortok, Repulse Bay

If you observe Rankin Inlet in winter and spring, you can see that contaminants are carried via the sewage system to the sea. The raw sewage is spilled directly into the harbour 365 days a year and this directly affects the food chain. There are two rivers that fish use to get down to the bay and which are very close to where the sewage is dumped. The fish migrating through those rivers could be carrying some of the contamination. Cod,

sculpins, shrimp, and smaller fish are directly affected if the food they eat has been contaminated. Some of them may even eat the waste. The canoes and boats are getting dirty from sewage.

Jack Angoo, Whale Cove

The scientists have said contaminants settle inside Hudson Bay, where we know they are carried by animals like fish, seals, and fish-eating birds. It doesn't matter where you are in the system because sea mammals use currents to travel everywhere, and leave the bay through Hudson Strait. The contaminants are also carried by the air. This contamination is not visible to the naked eye, but it is not good for our bodies. All kinds of contaminants like methyl-mercury are created when man disturbs the ecosystem by building dikes or dams, and making huge reservoirs. The microscopic organisms eat the contaminants, then fish get it from eating these tiny organisms. Seals and fish-eating birds eat the fish and, finally, humans eat the fish, seals, and fish-eating birds.

Lucassie Arragutainaq, Sanikiluaq

The animals taste different now than they did in the past, and it is not only due to the pollution in the earth. It is also pollution in the atmosphere that comes from steel plants and other factories. The pollutants rise to the air and are brought over here by the wind. Recently, I have started noticing that when it rains a lot, the puddles have something yellow floating in them. This comes from the sky brought down by the rain. It sticks to the earth and soil and so it affects the animals that feed from the plant life. The trees are also affected by this air pollution especially the birch, which is being destroyed at a very fast pace.

Alec Weistche, Waskaganish

There was oil and fuel in the muskeg when we came from Gillam with the 'dozers in the spring of 1989. There were many geese on that trail and they were feeding on the roots right where the oil was. Sometimes, there was 30 in a group and many of them were oily. They taste the way they do because they eat polluted plants.

Stanley Redhead, Shamattawa

56

Health effects

We've been told not to eat seal liver anymore due to possible contamination. However, we continue to eat fresh seal liver as soon as we open the seal because we can't change our way of life. We know very well we've been told not to eat too much of our country foods, but we have not slowed down eating them. How can we?

Lucassie Iqaluk, Inukjuak

Human bodies stay alive by eating food. If we don't eat we starve to death. We become weak by not eating well. Nowadays, we have started to hear our natural foods are contaminated by chemicals like methyl-mercury or PCBs. They say that they are aware of the contaminants which are now in our food systems. One time, there was this person who was gathering animal names to do research on our natural food system. He said that the birds coming in from further south contain contaminants when they arrive. These are birds we like to eat. Also, they talk about the seals carrying PCBs in their fat; all the larger mammals carry PCBs and other contaminants. That, too, is food which we depend on.

Moses Novalinga, Sanikiluaq

All the mercury testing and talk about safe levels make people afraid. They hear these things, but they do not understand what is happening in their body.

Donald Saunders, York Landing

Garbage

The rivers became polluted with all kinds of garbage as the communities got larger.

Peter Audlaluk, Ivujivik

As a hunter, it is very ugly when you see garbage lying around while you are out. The garbage affects animals so when I go out I bring it back to the community. It is one of the things that drives away the animals. It is not good for the animals. There are thousands of empty oil drums lying around all over the place, and those are very damaging to the environment.

Joshua Sala, Umiujaq

Whenever we see garbage left behind by campers or hunters we tend to raise a fuss and complain about it all the time so people focus their minds on it! We go through the radio letting the people know about local hunting policies and all the rules, including don't forget to bring your garbage from hunting or camping trips back to the community.

Peter Audlaluk, Ivujivik

Long ago, the river shores looked very beautiful when we went inland. Today, there is a lot of scrap metal that has been left behind by the white man. You see metal wire and gas drums in the water turning the sand brown every place that the white man has been working. He has worked in many areas and just leaves his garbage and oil drums on the river shorelines. I ask, what [are] the metal wire and oil and gas drums doing to the fish? I don't think [they're] doing the fish any good. [They're] hurting them. One of the camps along the river shore had a building made entirely of metal that was bulldozed into the river. When its metal starts corroding underwater how much damage will it do?

Alec Weistche, Waskaganish

Our animal foods are changing too. Rabbits, birds, and snow geese are not worth eating when they're inside the community and you've seen them in dumps. We don't want to eat them when they're eating from the dump because they're eating things they didn't eat before. My wife, for example, loves rabbit meat but doesn't want to eat it anymore because she saw one eating near the garbage barrel. And, the geese are too tame to eat now. The birds, especially snow geese, are in the dumps and sewage lagoons a lot. Everything is changing, and they're eating what isn't part of their normal diets. Polar bears eat plastic, garbage, and motor oil to keep something in their stomachs when they don't have any other food. Caribou drink from the sewage lagoons sometimes.

Peter Alogut, Coral Harbour; Simeonie Akpik, Lake Harbour

Radar installations

We happened to be in the path of the Mid-Canada radar line so quick developments took place there for the protection of Canada. It took about five years to construct the site and it only operated for ten years. Everything that had been brought there was left behind as junk when it closed. All kinds of stuff like liquid nitrogen, acid, and electrical transformers were left behind. About ten years later, they came to check if there was anything wrong at those sites. Environmental studies were done, and they found out that most of us who worked there had PCBs in our system.

Louis Bird, Peawanuck

They had [these] sites every 50 kilometres between 1950 and 1960. When they shut our base down they left everything behind. The energy building has 15 or 20 bottles of carbon dioxide and people have been letting this stuff out. Oil was spilled into the soil. There was no place to store used oil so they just dumped it on the ground and it eventually got into the rivers and lakes. Fish died from it. I don't know how many 24-volt batteries they used but acid was spilled into the soil too. The acid has a long lifetime and destroys the environment but they just dumped the batteries outside instead of destroying them elsewhere. They had anywhere from four to six 5000-gallon tanks at every site. There is still lots of equipment and buildings at those sites including 350-foot [107-metre] high towers with a satellite dish on top, caterpillars, graders, tractors, radios, carbon dioxide bottles, and waste that has affected the wildlife.

Western Hudson Bay Cree

Wildlife management

Traditional Cree and Inuit have trouble translating the scientific concept of wildlife management into their languages. During the second study workshop they explained that, to them, the word "management" implies control over animals, yet they believe it is not possible to have control over animals in the wilderness. They are taught that humans do not have power over animals and that it is disrespectful to act as though you do have power and dominance over nature. When Inuit and Cree go out on the land they hunt what they need, not all that they could get.

Inuit and Cree also often disagree with how wildlife biologists treat, handle, and manage wildlife:

Scientists and wildlife managers don't realize the damage they do to the animals or birds they try to study. They don't realize that they are mistreating the environment when their study or policy interferes with the life of a bird or animal.

Jimmy Rupert, Chisasibi

They have different excuses for why they study the animals, but it comes down to only one reason—money. With our knowledge, we can identify whether an animal is sick or not but they want to make money from learning about our animals. That is the kind of knowledge they want. They only seem to study the animals when it is profitable to them in some way. As Inuit, we are totally different from the white man and don't see the animals as money. We see them as food. We kill an animal to eat it, and have good reasons for why we don't like to eat what has been put to sleep [i.e., tranquillized for study, then released]. This is our way of life. We grow up with the animals here in the north, so we would appreciate it if they wouldn't do that.

Peter Alogut, Coral Harbour

I'm going to explain a bit about our Elders disagreeing with what scientists do, that is, finding geese and putting collars around their necks. So many times, the Elders found those geese hanging up on the little willows during their trapping. They're very furious about that. There is also when they go after the polar bears to check them. They use a tranquillizing gun, work on them, and then let them go. Hunters find the polar bears hurt and infected from the sharp tranquillizer. The polar bears begin to get weak and skinny and, later on, the hunters find them dead. The Elders think that this is a sin against nature. It shouldn't be done at all. To them, it's a really bad thing to do. Also, down south they have a policy for fishermen that says: "Do not kill the fish that is not the right weight or exact size." They let it go and the next thing they know, they find dead fish. These fish

are dead after they've been thrown away. It is the same thing with counting eggs. Our Elders instruct us never to touch eggs when they are being laid in the nest because, if we touch them, the geese usually just leave them. That was a very powerful teaching when we were young. But the people who study the geese go in there and count the eggs, mark them and everything. All of a sudden, the geese just leave their eggs there. That's what makes our people unhappy.

Louis Bird, Peawanuck

As they have with many other aspects of their lives today, Hudson Bay Cree and Inuit find it challenging to maintain traditional systems of using, handling, and treating wildlife:

The government took over our animals, and started making laws according to the knowledge of scientists and wildlife officers. They make laws without listening to us even though we have our own traditional knowledge of the environment and wildlife. It's not surprising we're never satisfied with the laws they make because we already have our own knowledge of the animals. There are so many pages that we have to follow according to the government laws.

Lucassie Arragutainaq, Sanikiluaq

We may shoot five geese a day according to the rules and regulations from the game warden. But, it is really difficult to follow our traditional way of keeping track of the wounded animals and fulfilling rules from the game warden. For instance, once I was a guide for two white hunters and, although they shot many geese, they could only pick up five each. The rest of the wounded fell some distance away. We couldn't go and take those because of our fear of the Ministry of Natural Resources and the game warden, who checks your bags and canoe when you get to the community.

Stanley Thomas, Fort Severn

Marine mammal issues

Today, they are saying marine species are diminishing in numbers because we hunt too many, but that is not so. Our wildlife management system has changed from the past. People harvested more in the past than they do now because dogs and family groups had to be considered. We used to kill and store enough food for winter in order to feed the dog teams we used for transportation.

Peter Alogut, Coral Harbour; Simeonie Akpik, Lake Harbour

The mussels, especially, multiply more when they are being harvested. Also, I wish they could stop saying that the whales are decreasing in numbers. The Inuit people still believe that the animals will always show up even if you don't see them in a particular area for a long time. Inuit know about that, but the Renewable Resource people keep telling us that the animals are decreasing in numbers. They can even tell you how many animals there are, but nobody knows how many animals are really left. In our traditional knowledge, when you use the animals according to their purpose, they will always prosper and reproduce themselves as you need them. We can never believe it when we're told the animals are decreasing because we know how the animals and environment work up here. We also know any living being will cease to exist when the time comes. Today, our food is here for us to use as it was planned in the first place.

Peter Alogut, Coral Harbour; Simeonie Akpik, Lake Harbour

Sport hunting and fishing

We had a lot of people from the south caribou hunting, especially in the past couple of years. The government has a lottery where you enter your name, and if they pick it you have the right to go hunting caribou. A lot of things have happened since this lottery started. Basically, it has had a devastating impact because, as you know, you need a very large territory when you hunt. You also have to let the land rest. You can't overhunt an area.

Helen Atkinson, Chisasibi

Also, these sport hunters hunt from their trucks and some people are very scared to drive down the road now. They see these hunters with their guns by the windows, shooting at caribou. A lot of times, these hunters just take a small part of the animal and leave the rest to rot which our hunters find very sad to see. It's the same thing even with

the fish. If the fish is too small for them, they just leave it on the shore. A friend of mine, whose camp is inland, says it's now full of white people. They're coming with their "Winnebagos" and make it like a parking lot. Some of the camps are broken into; things are broken and stolen. One person's canoe was sitting on the land and somebody drove his truck into it so the canoe is totally smashed. Their cabin was broken into; all the windows broken. They used the stuff that was inside the house and left beer cans and liquor bottles all over the place. The people said, "We just turned around and came back. We didn't want to even look at it."

Helen Atkinson, Chisasibi

I did some guiding for two seasons of sport fishing. I think they enjoy just casting their rod. Their purpose is not necessarily to get the fish to eat like we do. Often they throw the fish back in the water after it's caught even if it's injured inside the mouth. I've seen them use clamps that they put right into the mouth of fish to pull out the hook. That's one thing I don't agree with myself because if they injure the inside of the fish then it will bleed into the stomach. The fish will eventually go into a little bay and die because it was hurt. This business of catching a fish and putting it back into the water creates employment but it also damages the environment, water, and fish. There are fewer fish in the sport fishing areas, and the catch limits are reduced when that happens. So, I say, when you catch and release, you are really catching and damaging. It's a money thing I suppose but you have to try to preserve the water and the fish that are living in it.

Jimmy Small, Moose Factory

Note

1. Hudson Bay TEKMS Workshop 1. 1992. Unpublished transcript. HBP: Sanikiluaq.

"What we never really hear about is the human impact.... All the studies are very specialized in studying the effects of development on certain physical things in the environment. There is really no complete picture of what it does to our people, the community, animals, and the whole environment."

Future Needs

Traditional ecological knowledge is rooted in a valued way of life that gives meaning to aboriginal existence. Any action threatening the integrity of traditional values demands careful assessment of the risk it adds to a community's ability to cope with and adjust to change. There are both thresholds and limits to the amount of change human and animal communities can sustain in highly variable environments over short periods of time.

It is clear that the Cree and Inuit of Hudson Bay need a sense of renewed ecological security. Specifically, they seek assurance that there will always be a healthy environment and land for future generations.

In the past, experience and knowledge were handed down from generation to generation, providing understanding and guidance to sustain life in a profoundly respected environment. Today's Elders try to continue this tradition but, in their lifetime, they have experienced *outsiders* taking control of almost every aspect of their lives—including their children's education, their economy, lands, rivers, and the way they can hunt, trap, and use the animals. They see their next generation trying to deal with cross-cultural problems stemming from two very different views of the environment. Contaminants, hydroelectric utilities, roads, logging, mining, and land and wildlife management are all provoking problems that underscore the fundamental need for a renewed sense of cultural and ecological security.

For the past 10 to 20 years, Elders have encouraged younger generations to *bring together the best from both cultures*. Traditional Cree and Inuit are now asking some tough questions: With all the environmental changes occurring and pressures for Cree and Inuit to change, what will become of the next generation? What problems will be encountered? What *insurance* is there for their cultural survival?

Recognition

As Inuit and Cree, we don't want to give up our beliefs, and we don't want to surrender what we believe in to southern developers.

Simeonie Akpik, Lake Harbour

The reason we cannot keep from voicing our opinions and observations comes from seeing that our homeland and hunting areas are now unable to support us.... We cannot do anything for the water and the land that we have lost through flooding. It is gone for good. We will never see it as it once was. We can only hope that the Creator will help us in our struggle to heal the land, the animals and ourselves.

William Fireman, Chisasibi; Joseph Petagumskum, Whapmagoostui

We have told them many times that what we and our Ancestors survived on, in the hunting field, is disappearing.... They do not heed the advice given to them.... Look at the fish and what is happening to them. Much more will happen to life on the land. The effects [from the dams] are far-reaching.... The white man has to realize that all this destruction is wreaking havoc on all life out on the land and that it has far-reaching effects.

John Matches, Wemindji

The environment must remain healthy because people have to rely on it for food.... Some of the foods have already been damaged. That is the reason why the river system has to be left alone by the developers. ... some big contaminants will be discharged when they flood land for the reservoir. ... the contaminants will accumulate over the years, and that's why I am worried for my next generations.

Johnny Kavik, Sanikiluaq; Simon Makimmak, Akulivik

Some people have no more drinking water, not to mention the fish which are being destroyed. Also, the ducks and geese have had to change their travel routes because of alteration in their feeding habitats. Every part of our environment has been affected by developments, and that includes humans. Our own culture should not be next to be damaged.

Quitsak Tarkiasuk, Ivujivik

We love our lands. We also love our animals. Our own culture is priceless. We don't want to lose our culture.

Quitsak Tarkiasuk, Ivujivik

63

A healthy environment

Rivers and lakes contribute a lot to the well-being of people. You cannot make a decent living from land that has no water on it. The currents and rivers are the veins of Hudson Bay. They start from inside the basin and go out through Hudson Strait. If any part of the currents or rivers are altered in Hudson Bay, the basin will start to slowly die ... and the animals will die with it.

George Diamond, Sr., Waskaganish; Peter Kattuk, Sanikiluaq

Cree and Inuit may have different cultures but one thing we think alike on is preservation of the animals and environment. We preserve the environment because it is the place where we hunt the animals for food. If we're going to live a good life, our environment has to be clean. The animals can't live in a dirty area because they go bad. It's the same for us ... because we're among the living, and we're part of the environment.

Lucassie Arragutainaq, Sanikiluaq

Monitoring

The world's environment evolves daily. There are changes which occur every day. If somebody could keep up with this world, we would know every detail of it.

Johnny Epoo, Inukjuak

We have to watch carefully once they start releasing the freshwater from the new generating station near Chisasibi because our floe edge started completely freezing over the last ten or so years. So, we will have to watch Belcher Islands' sea-ice area.

Peter Kattuk, Sanikiluaq

There's going to be a great change in the water temperature of Hudson Bay itself [if the Great Whale hydroelectric development goes ahead]. And this is where they will notice the environmental impact.

John Petagumskum, Whapmagoostui

Various small bird species like phalaropes, sandpipers, and Arctic tern used to be abundant during their spring migration. These smaller bird species depend on organisms to feed. They also

dwell in very polluted areas. They really help clean the polluted areas and ponds. I've noticed they have decreased in numbers on Southampton Island since my childhood.

Peter Alogut, Coral Harbour

Traditional foods

We want our traditional diets to be respected.

John Petagumskum, Whapmagoostui

We have to work very hard keeping our fresh foods available because we are in the north, where you cannot farm due to harsh conditions.

Joshua Sala, Umiujaq

As I grew up and began to stay in the community my life changed. Because my diet consisted of processed foods, I began to notice I was getting weak. So were my children because they were eating what was available in the community. When I returned to the bush, and started eating the food I grew up with, I noticed my children and I began to improve our health.

Gabriel Fireman, Attawapiskat

I find the same thing myself. If I don't eat traditional food for a long time I don't feel as healthy.... With traditional food we find we are more healthy.

Edward Tapiatic, Chisasibi

Country food makes your blood pure which makes your body strong.

Joshua Sala, Umiujaq

The [white man's] food tires you very easily. When we were eating only country foods, we did not get tired. We used to work all day. There was no such thing as getting tired.

Mina Weetaltuk, Kuujjuaraapik

Traditional ecological knowledge

I now understand that the ones who do live off the land are the ones telling how it's really like. ... we have very good knowledge and, if we use our knowledge, there would be a lot of scientific knowledge....

Edward Tapiatic, Chisasibi; Lucassie Arragutainaq, Sanikiluaq

We should not depend just on southern expertise. Our traditional knowledge has value to be shared with the South. Wildlife scientists and southern politicians are the architects who introduced wildlife legislation. But, we have to be actively involved too. There has to be a balance of information in terms of the environment and wildlife. Inuit [and Cree] traditional knowledge will have to be part of the process.

Lucassie Arragutainaq, Sanikiluaq

The Elders are the ones that are the scientists and professionals in our land. So, when I hear Hydro or a scientist say, "Their facts are all wrong, they don't know what they did," it disappoints me.... [white people] have their experts and our experts are the Elders. We should be comparing the knowledge of those two.

Edward Tapiatic, Chisasibi; Louis Bird, Peawanuck

When we are told by our Elders that something will happen, it is because they are aware of something that is way ahead in the future. All our lives we have listened to the knowledge of our Elders just like others did before us. We are still listening to the knowledge of our Elders, today. They know when our animals are moving further away because their Elders knew. They know when there's not going to be many animals. Some of us have the same knowledge now.... We have much knowledge and it is worth keeping.

Jack Angoo, Whale Cove

Cultural education

From teaching traditional knowledge, comes a way of living that preserves harmony, and does not disrupt or damage the environment or animals.

Unknown

I know about animals since I grew up hunting in the land and water. I've seen so many of them throughout the years.... I know about caribou: where they go, and where they stay in the winter. Long before the government took over our animals, and even long before we had our kids, my wife and I used to travel a lot throughout the land: hunting, and providing ourselves with country food. We did this because my wife's parents used to tell us to go out on the land so we could learn and provide for ourselves. They wanted us to learn how to survive amongst ourselves so we can teach the younger generation when we're old.

Andy Mamgark, Arviat

We received our cultural education from our Elders who passed it on verbally, and by example. Everything that we presently have to live in our land was passed down from our Elders. It is part of the education system in our culture.... Our fathers knew how to use and preserve all these things, how to take care of them, and how to make best use of them. All that is included in our cultural education.

Gabriel Fireman, Attawapiskat

... young people should be taught not only the white man's way. They should also be learning the ways of their own Ancestors and the way of life they survived on.... In our community the young people are taught only the hunting activities that go on in summer.... They do not see what their father and mother do out on the land in winter.... They will not have the skills of their fathers and grandfathers. When the changes come to the land and water, they will be very poor indeed.... Much of the Cree culture has now been discontinued and that is why the young people will be poor when they try being out on the land on their own.

George Diamond, Sr., Waskaganish

Our people, at that time, were aware of slow changes. I am, today, well aware what it does to

us and know that to resist is not the answer.... Once we realized how it affects our children by sending them down South for schooling, we decided to establish our own community high school system which will be equivalent to other high school education.... Today, because we include our culture in the education system, our young people are beginning to realize and understand what effects a major development will have on our traditional way of life. By studying the history of our community, and our cultural background, our young people have a better understanding of the importance of maintaining our culture. Today, those who have acquired education and knowledge of both cultures have a better understanding of the Elders' point of view in terms of land use. Because our young people now speak English, they understand the major development issues. They now know what land inheritance means....

Gabriel Fireman, Attawapiskat

Development planning

How much will the land be damaged before they realize they're damaging the whole population of Hudson Bay and James Bay? Is it government? Is it Hydro?... There must be somebody involved that gives them the land to do all this stuff. I think it's time the government, Hydro, or other officials we deal with realize that they have to understand what we do, and what they're doing to us.

Jimmy Small, Moose Factory

We already know that more dams are in the making, and they are planning to put up a dike at the mouth of James Bay to export freshwater. This is a long-term plan that has to be looked at. I think the native people should know more, and ahead of time, if anything is to be done in their community or wherever they use the land.... There wasn't much said about what was going to happen at the time of the first James Bay project. They just spoke more or less of work, and creating jobs for native people. We were more concerned about our daily life, where we lived, and never thought about the future of the dams.

Edward Tapiatic, Chisasibi

Some development projects ... may be beneficial to our communities employment-wise.... However, even though they may be of dollar value, we also have to look at their damaging effects in order to select those projects which come our way. We also look to the future in terms of what will benefit our children. To this end, our Elders are aware of upcoming projects. They know what they will cause, and what will change further. They know of long-term changes by nature as well as human-caused changes.

Louis Bird, Peawanuck

Suppose future developers listen to us, and ask if they can do some work in our lands. I know we can stop them, but they will always try starting all over again. They will just wait awhile then try again when they think we have forgotten or are getting soft. They will always tell you that there will be no damages when we know our food sources will be damaged.

Simeonie Akpik, Lake Harbour

We used to use our voice without written agreements. This whole thing which we are talking about should be done only through written agreements with the developers or governments.... Any developer who wants to explore in the North should first ask the communities who will be directly affected by the developments. They should inform the communities before they start their planning, and then explore anything that may become a concern to the affected areas. This is necessary because more and more developers are going ahead without letting us know....

Mathewsie Sakiagaq, Kangiqsujuaq; Lucassie Arragutainaq, Sanikiluaq; Simeonie Akpik, Lake Harbour

Our lands have a lot of minerals just waiting to be discovered. Through different agreements, some of our organizations and people are even part of the mining activities now. We do things like explore the lands for minerals so we are part of the process. Although we may not have the power to stop such developments, we have to state our concerns. Things have to be planned beforehand, and we have to put our policies in order so we can have better environments.... We should make policies or guidelines beforehand so things can also work out for us in the future.... The only possible solution is for better management of the whole development process by having agreements with the companies based on what we know as well.

Noah Isaac, Salluit; Mathewsie Sakiagaq, Kangiqsujuaq

We must value our cultural system in dollar terms so we can negotiate, or at least speak, in the same terms with the government.... To them, when we resist major development, we are resisting what would be more beneficial for us. That's their whole point of view. Our point is: We will not be included in the revenue that is being taken from the underground resources. Since we are approaching self-government—and we did not give up the land—we should have the rights to the resources. We are aiming to share the resources which will help us maintain our self-government structure.

Louis Bird, Peawanuck

Conservation

As Inuit and aboriginal people of the land, we should have more say in the management of wild animals ... because [we] are the ones with the knowledge. The Elders ... passed the knowledge which they have used for a long time....

Donat Milortok, Repulse Bay

As an Inuk, it hurts to see animals being mistreated because we know that they are our only food, and our future generations will depend on them for food too.... For that reason, alone, those animals have to be handled properly. If a white man decides to destroy them he says, "we will compensate you for them." But, even if their compensation is big, the money will vanish. Our animals are our only source of food so they should be handled wisely....

Donat Milortok, Repulse Bay

If we start thinking that we are superior to the animals things can go wrong. We have to be very careful how we decide about our animals, or anything that belongs to nature. We have to say things right and be true every time we talk about our nature. If you start guessing, things can go very wrong.

Lucassie Iqaluk, Inukjuak

Future research

The Southerners usually just go ahead with whatever they are planning because they have the resources and money.... But, they cannot go ahead as planned if a group of people don't agree with their intentions. ... then there has to be research....

Peter Matte, Akulivik

We must study together so we know how to share the land. We both have questions, and maybe we could take our colleagues' scientific information back to our communities. Maybe scientists can benefit from traditional knowledge....

Louis Bird, Peawanuck

... all the transmission lines that carry the power to the South have a large effect on the environment and our lives too. We have a serious problem with them, but Hydro-Québec has never sat down with us to explain the effects of these transmission lines.

Robbie Matthews, Chisasibi

One of our concerns, as people from Sanikiluaq, Belcher Islands, is that whenever there is hydroelectric damming, researchers do their studies inland and I don't think they ever do research at the mouth of the rivers or even in Hudson Bay.

Zack Novalinga, Sanikiluaq

Another thing ... is what effect warm temperatures have on the fish when combined with low water levels in summer?

Donald Saunders, York Landing

We, as a group, know where the fish are and which lakes contain fish of different kinds. These names could also be included in the [research] because if any lake is affected by development, lots of fish are in danger of being affected too. ... we have to expect a long-term effect.

Donat Milortok, Repulse Bay

Wildlife studies

There seem to be two types of studies: one is location of the animal, and they put radios on them to do that. That kind of study is totally not linked to our way of life, and we don't really agree with it. The other study is where they take and study the meat or fat of the animals. They send away the meat and fat, and study it, to see if the white man has created sickness in those animals. I like it when the white man studies the animals to see what he, himself, has done to them.

John Kaunak, Repulse Bay

We had no say when the government started doing the first kind of study.... The only time they want something to do with us is when they want our help. Our wildlife officers ask for our help when they want something done to the animal, and we do give them what they ask for. Still, we never hear what the results are nor what caused the animal to be that way. We're just giving and giving without getting anything back. Give us the results of those studies, and let us understand too.

John Kaunak, Repulse Bay

If we were told in advance why they are doing studies which make the animals suffer so much I think it would be a lot better. So everybody understands what's happening. Biologists do just come and go for their studies without informing the communities.... I really would like to get the information on why they do a study, and what kind of drugs they use to put the animal under their control. I am sure the animal meat is not natural once they have been put to sleep.

Simeonie Akpik, Lake Harbour

Cree and Inuit find the way polar bears are tranquillized and handled by wildlife biologists very offensive and highly disrespectful, and they question whether polar bears have to be *mishandled* for scientists to get the information they seek. They also wonder if working with knowledgeable Cree and Inuit might help wildlife specialists learn what they need to know about polar bears, without causing the suffering and loss of natural abilities that result from tranquillizing, tagging, tattooing, and removing teeth.

All the communities which we met with around James and Hudson bays have said, "don't touch the animals. Don't put them to sleep. Tell the government to stop their biologists from doing their studies if they are going to make the animals suffer."

Lucassie Arragutainaq, Sanikiluaq

Working together

The knowledge of our Elders is even more important today, especially with big industrial companies and governments aggressively wishing to exploit our land. As aboriginal people, we have long relied on the land for our survival. We cannot, nor should we, be forced to stop using the land today or in the future. We are proud of our Elders' efforts. We have always depended on [them] for guidance and, today, it is evident we will still turn towards [them] for [their] wisdom.

Mikidjuk Kolola, Lake Harbour

The environment has no boundaries. We will have to support each other whether we are Inuit, Cree, white people or other people.

Titi Kadluk, Chesterfield Inlet

You probably cannot totally stop all the developments around Hudson Bay. But, the people who live around the bay have to work together. We need to keep in touch with each other to plan for our future and to share some of our concerns when it comes to dealing with what is going to affect our lives.

Johnny Epoo, Inukjuak

O' Lord ... the work we are doing is for us to agree on things so we can live better lives. We are asking you to give us a hand in taking care of the animals so they can last.... So we can use them for food. We are also asking you to let us ... be part of the plans for our animals. Also, help the people even though they are planning to damage your land, and help us to work with the people who are planning to destroy your lands, so we can reach an agreement with them. That's the only way to work things out. Also, give us strength to work with the white people so some day they will understand us and start working with us. In this case, and for our animals' sake, we are praying to you O' God.

Simeonie Akpik, Lake Harbour

Afterword

We still don't have all the information about the real traditional values that are connected to our wildlife and environment. Some of [those values] are still very useful for a better living. [They] help to put the mind at ease. Maybe, we're too young to know of the real way of Inuit life but, from what we have heard, we can try to see if [the information] could still be used today. We're losing our Inuit way of life very fast [but] we still have information that could slow this down. So, if we [can make that a priority] it would at least try to prevent the loss of knowledge about our wildlife and anything else. We can still improve our situation now, if we can find a way ... to prevent those losses.

John Kaunak, Repulse Bay

Since we started meeting as a group, our words have spread and are being heard. They are now starting to be understood.... I believe that [because] I'm hearing them now say, "we will try hard to protect your animals and find a way that's least damaging to the area." That's what the people who want to study rocks are now saying. I want us, as members of this project, to keep going.... We would like to see that and to be able to say we live here and this is our lifestyle. If we're going to keep informing them about this, it will be good.

Noah Isaac, Salluit

It is important to distribute these materials that we have put into writing. We should give them to the young people so they are informed of why our Elders sat here—the way they express things which they think are important. There seems to be a lot of subjects that have been put together in these workshops that would help our young people understand our purpose and determination to save our environment—what's left of it up North. We know that we cannot stop the major projects that will take place as the Europeans keep increasing in this land of ours. We will not be able to stop them. That is why we must educate our children to adjust more easily and faster than we do, but still not to lose our Ancestral respect of our land and environment, both spiritually and materially.... We have shown to each other how much we care for everything that is living or existing as animal, plant, element, liquid or solid rock.... We begin to understand how we value these things today and our children will come to understand much better if they see our effort. We are trying to do the best we can. This [is] why we say we should not allow our efforts in this Programme to be just put onto the shelves and forgotten. We should make sure [copies] exist in each community and for each group that is involved in the public, like politicians or even companies that are interested in our region. So they may understand what we are talking about. What we want them to know is how much we care for the place we live in, the land and everything.

Louis Bird, Peawanuck

Appendices

"We must educate our children to adjust more easily and faster than we do, but still not to lose our Ancestral respect of our land and environment, both spiritually and materially."

Appendix A: Hudson Bay Programme TEKMS Study Research Methodology

Research process and schedule

The Hudson Bay Traditional Ecological Knowledge Management Systems (TEKMS) study was designed to encourage the participation of interested communities and people. The chair of the Sanikiluaq Environmental Committee (who is also the Mayor of Sanikiluaq) initially wrote to the chief or mayor of some 30 communities in the region, inviting their participation.

Eight communities participated in the first workshop, held in October 1992, to discuss regional environmental concerns, identify study goals and research topics, and finalize a meeting schedule.

The research topics were organized to provide guidelines for a series of regional working group meetings that were hosted by eight communities.[1] Each host community invited its neighbouring communities and provided homes, meals, and hospitality during the meetings held between November 1992 and December 1993.

The research topics reflected deep concern among indigenous residents for the environment of Hudson and James bays:[2]

- **Environmental changes** in climate, water quality, marine currents, seasonal flow of dammed and diverted rivers, sea-ice formation, and shoreline habitat

- **Natural foods and traditional societies**
    - changes in natural food supply including quality, quantity, and availability
    - changes in natural drinking water quality and supply
    - effects of road salt on ptarmigan
    - effects of weakening currents and extended sea-ice cover on the Hudson Bay eider population
    - effects of weather and habitat changes, including disappearance of eel grass, on geese
    - effects of increased resource competition from non-traditional activities on access and use of traditional territories and on traditional management systems
    - increasing number of sick animals in eastern James Bay
    - increasing number of unexplained or unusual deaths, diseases, and illnesses, including allergies, among indigenous residents

- **Contamination**
    - impacts on sea-bottom organisms eaten year-round by sea mammals and people
    - diffusion of contaminants among wildlife including those that move in and out of Hudson Bay
    - bioaccumulation of methyl-mercury in fish, marine species, Cree, and Inuit

- **Hydroelectric development**
    - impacts of dams, diversions, and water regulation on rivers flowing into Hudson and James bays
    - lack of understanding on what hydroelectric development does to people, communities, environment, and animals living in Hudson and James bays
    - effects of altered river regimes on traditional activities and animal use
    - effects of reservoirs on climate, ice conditions, air temperature, and transportation
    - effects of transmission lines on humans, wildlife, and vegetation
    - cumulative effect on salinity balance, salt-water freezing, and sea-ice formation in Hudson and James bays

- **Forestry**
    - effects of clear-cutting on rivers flowing into Hudson and James bays

- **Future developments**
    - impacts on harvesting traditional foods

Seventy-eight participants—an average of two representatives from each community—shared and contributed valuable knowledge to the study. Most were either Elders or active hunters, and the average age was 56 years. The youngest contributor was 26 years, and the eldest, Mr. Joseph Saunders of the York Factory Cree Nation, was born in 1909.

A second set of working group meetings was held in autumn 1993 to verify knowledge recorded and mapped in the first meetings. Eighty-six per cent of the original contributors representing all but one community returned for the verification meetings, ensuring continuity between the two meetings and a common focus for the second study workshop.

Working Group	Participating Communities	Host
Northwestern Hudson Bay	Repulse Bay, Coral Harbour, Chesterfield Inlet, Whale Cove, Arviat	Chesterfield Inlet, Rankin Inlet
Hudson Strait	Cape Dorset, Lake Harbour, Kangiqsujuaq, Salluit, Ivujivik	Lake Harbour, Kangiqsujuaq
Eastern Hudson Bay	Akulivik, Inukjuak, Sanikiluaq, Umiujaq, Kuujjuaraapik	Sanikiluaq
Eastern James Bay	Waskaganish, Chisasibi, Wemindji, Whapmagoostui	Chisasibi
Western James Bay	Moose Factory (also includes community of Mont Creebec), Fort Albany, Kashechewan, Attawapiskat, Peawanuck	Moose Factory
Western Hudson Bay	Fort Severn, Shamattawa, York Landing	York Landing

The second study workshop was held in January 1994. Two representatives from each working group met to review system-wide TEKMS findings and to discuss future use of knowledge documented during the study.

A third workshop, held in April 1994, brought together scientists and regional TEKMS representatives to exchange information on some of the identified processes and changes occurring in the Hudson Bay ecosystem. It marked completion of Phase I of the Hudson Bay Programme.

Study methods

The working group meetings provided indigenous residents with the opportunity to discuss and document their knowledge of the environment in an empowering and respectful manner.

The meetings were organized and conducted by Hudson Bay Programme study and research co-ordinators with help from regional co-ordinators, language interpreters, and mapping technicians. Each meeting in the first set lasted four days and followed the same agenda—discussions on study purpose, weather, rivers, shorelines, currents, ice, animals, traditional management, human health, and effects of development. The meetings were conducted in four Cree dialects, three Inuttitut dialects, and English, with contributors using their language of preference.

The study and research co-ordinators met with an Elders' Advisory Committee in Sanikiluaq between meetings to discuss findings and clarify areas of inquiry. After completion of the first set of meetings, they also met with the TEKMS Technical Advisory Committee, composed of respected natural and social scientists from Canadian universities, institutes, and government departments, to review preliminary findings, discuss technical issues regarding organization of the TEKMS database, and receive advice on preparation for the verification meetings.

The verification meetings began in August 1993, after proceedings from the first set of meetings had been compiled and organized by the study team. Using a set of common themes and specific questions, each working group spent three days reviewing and clarifying information from maps, charts, and transcripts.

Meetings with members of the Technical Advisory Committee were held after the verification meetings to review map information for inclusion in Hudson Bay Programme reports and after the second study workshop for advice on the completion of study reports within the Phase I time framework.

Database development and processing

The Hudson Bay TEKMS study was designed in anticipation of large volumes of graphic and descriptive information. Geographic Information System (GIS) principles were applied in the study design so the information could be compiled, organized, analyzed, and reproduced in relation to specific geographic locations in the Hudson Bay bioregion. All 15 meeting proceedings were recorded on audio cassette, then translated and transcribed into English. Meeting notes, flip charts, and guidelines were also transcribed into source documents. As well, community representatives spent one day in their first meeting recording traditional ecological knowledge on map overlays for integration with text and other attribute information into a GIS.

Development of digital text database

The text database was organized on a Windows-based computer system using four main software programmes—MS-Word (word processing), SmarText (hypertext), Corel Draw (graphics), and MS-Excel (tables).

The primary source documents comprise approximately 1800 pages translated and transcribed from 114 sixty-minute audio tapes. Secondary source documents include meeting guidelines, notes, map overlay text, figures, and tables.

To ensure integrity of the original source documents, the cassettes and translations have been archived and cross-referenced, and the transcripts stored as "read only" documents in a separate computer directory.

Working copies of each English-language transcript, made from the original "read only" documents, were converted into MS-Word to allow light editing for clarification and standardization for input as source documents into SmarText. (SmarText is a hypertext software programme that enables users to move quickly from one part of an electronic document to another; allows direct use of source information to organize, compile, and report TEK by theme or problem definition; and copies information for word-processing functions without altering the content of original documents.)

Three main SmarText documents developed for the study report were the basis for compiling traditional knowledge from around Hudson and James bays and for synthesizing information for a system-wide review of processes and changes occurring in the ecosystem. The first document contains the six "lightly edited" transcripts from the first set of meetings. The second document contains the six "original" transcripts from the verification meetings. The third document contains transcripts and proceedings from the three study workshops. A common index developed for the three documents allowed each to be reviewed by conducting a combination of keyword searches that were relevant to a particular theme or topic of inquiry.

Development of digital map database

During the study, more than 110 map overlays of the TEK themes were produced by the working groups.

This map information was organized into a GIS database by the Natural Resources Secretariat of the Manitoba Keewatinowi Okimakanak (NRS-MKO), under contract to the Hudson Bay Programme (HBP).[3]

Map overlay information was recorded on base maps in six different scales: 1:50,000; 1:250,000; 1:500,000; 1:1,000,000; 1:4,000,000; and 1:4,055,040. In most cases, the map overlay information was hand drawn by its original contributor and descriptive notations were added by meeting facilitators to assist identification and analysis during database development.

In general, the map overlay information relates to rivers, shorelines, sea ice, currents, animals, and human activity. Each overlay, however, represents multiple TEK themes from several contributors. As a result, the digital map database contains information on the following nine elements:

1. Seasonal locations, migratory travel routes, and riverine, freshwater, terrestrial, and marine habitat for bird, fish, and animal populations including

   - waterfowl: Canada geese, snow geese, brants, ducks
   - freshwater fish: sturgeon, whitefish, dore, pike, pickerel, brook trout, lake trout, suckers
   - terrestrial species: moose, caribou, beaver, muskrat, fox, ptarmigan, rabbit
   - migratory species: ptarmigan, caribou, polar bear, harbour seal
   - anadromous species: Arctic char
   - marine species: walrus, beluga, ringed seal, capelin

2. Coastal shoreline features and changes including emerging shoals and islands

3. Surface tidal and current characteristics in marine waters and river estuaries

4. Wind directions

5. Sea-ice conditions including changes in floe-edge locations and polynyas

6. Places of cultural importance or geographical significance (i.e., burial sites, rivers, traditional travel routes, coastal and inland fishing spots, family hunting and trapping territories, camps, cabins, land-claims areas, and traditional place names)

7. Natural areas and features directly affected and altered by hydroelectric development including flooded rivers and lands, spawning rapids, estuaries, river and coastal shorelines

8. Human activities that are altering the natural environment, including current and proposed hydroelectric development (i.e., reservoirs, generating stations, work camps, accumulated garbage) and abandoned radar installations with buildings, radar equipment, oil and gas tanks

9. Forest fire sites

Organization

The map overlay information from each working group meeting was sent to NRS-MKO offices in Winnipeg, Manitoba, and Saskatoon, Saskatchewan, to be organized into a database, using *TerraSoft* (GIS software that enables recording, management, analysis, and reproduction of large volumes of both object [graphic] and attribute [descriptive] information in relation to specific geographic locations).[4]

Base maps and map overlay information were digitized at the original scale and analyzed to determine distinct TEK themes. The resulting GIS files were carefully compared, on a light table, with the original map overlay information to ensure the reproductions were faithful.

The resulting database, comprising more than 140 different TEK themes, is stored in 433 individual GIS files. It has been initially organized by TEK theme and community group.

Production of draft maps

NRS-MKO produced four series of maps, representing more than 90 individual map sheets, from TEK compiled during working group meetings and the second study workshop.

Series 1 reproduced all line work contained on map overlays from the first set of meetings. It was initially generated in 1:500,000 scale for analysis by HBP staff and use in the second set of meetings.

Series 2, again produced at 1:500,000 scale, incorporated revisions suggested by HBP and NRS-MKO staff to the first map series to facilitate review and verification by community representatives during the second set of meetings.

Series 3 incorporated results of the verification meetings and additional refinements suggested during the mapping meeting with the TEKMS Technical Advisory Committee. It consisted of seven representative TEK theme groups selected by HBP and NRS-MKO staff based on advice received from the Technical Advisory Committee. Produced for use during the second study workshop, the maps integrated information from the six working groups to enable system-wide understanding and analysis. This entailed copying and merging the GIS database into 60 GIS files to produce a series of system maps at a unified scale of 1:2,000,000.

Three "regional" maps of river mouth areas—the Nelson River, the Moose River, and La Grande River—were also produced as part of this series.

Series 4 incorporated additional information, changes, and refinements identified in the second study workshop and following detailed discussions between the HBP research co-ordinator and NRS-MKO project staff in April 1994.

Production of this particular series of seven system maps was part of the technical process in assembling system and regional GIS maps suitable for reproduction in various HBP reports. It required additional "merging" of the 60 GIS files from the third map series into 21 GIS files. Changing the base map working scale from 1:500,000 to 1:2,000,000 required modifications to all fonts and symbols to ensure legibility and special procedures to create maps within the Transverse Mercator projection at a uniform scale of 1:2,000,000.

Notes

1. Twenty-eight communities participated in the working group meetings. Whapmagoostui participated in the eastern James Bay working group meeting although its traditional land-use and occupancy area is in eastern Hudson Bay. Likewise, Peawanuck participated in the western James Bay working group although its traditional land-use and occupancy area is in southwestern Hudson Bay.

2. Hudson Bay TEKMS Workshop 1. 1992. Unpublished transcript. HBP: Sanikiluaq.

3. MKO is the Cree regional organization in northwestern Manitoba. NRS has applied GIS to TEK and traditional land-use research since 1989.

4. GIS differs from the Computer Assisted Design and Drafting (CADD) software often used in map production in that it is able to produce maps with real-world map references embedded and linked to a display of attributes organized in a database.

Appendix B: Seasonal Characteristics in Hudson Bay

Season	Location	Months	Characteristics
Early Fall *ukiaksak*	Ivujivik Salluit Kangiqsujuaq Lake Harbour Cape Dorset	Part September, part October September, October, part November September Part September, October September, October	Mature birds fly after moulting; young birds are ready to fly Air temperature drops; frost occurs; air colder every day Snow geese arrive from the north Caribou shed their antler skin Arctic char migrate upriver Seals start to fatten Ice forms in ponds, lakes, and rivers
makwa nipin	Peawanuck Kashechewan Fort Albany Moose Factory	Part September, part October Mid-September to 2nd wk October Mid-September to 2nd wk October September	Leaves fall from the trees
wipich tikwaachin	Waskaganish	September	Snow geese have not yet flown south Frost on the tree branches and ground Caribou become fat and prepare for mating
ukiaksak	Belcher Islands	September, October	Rains more frequently, ice pellet showers Days get shorter
	Inukjuak	September, October, part November	Much cooler air temperatures More west wind; winds and snow increasingly frequent
	Akulivik	October	Freezing rain, snow Lakes frozen: ice and net fishing Seal hunting
Fall *ukiaq*	Ivujivik Salluit Kangiqsujuaq Lake Harbour Cape Dorset	Part October, November Part November, December October, November Part October, November Part October, November, December	Snow falls, lakes and land freeze Sea ice starts to form in inlets and small bays Animal fur thickens, changes to white on some animals Caribou move together and mate Beluga whale and seal migrate to winter locations Walrus move inshore
ukiaksaaq	Coral Harbour Repulse Bay Chesterfield Inlet	September, October September, October September, October	Cooler air temperatures, blowing snow Sea ice forms inside inlets; land starts to freeze Hunters prepare and repair equipment for winter
eh ta koh kik	York Factory Fort Severn	Last part August, September Last part August, September	Mature birds are ready to fly after moulting Young birds are ready to fly for first time Geese are flying by August 20 Caribou and moose in mating seasons in September
tukwakin	Peawanuck Kashechewan Fort Albany Moose Factory	2nd wk October to 2nd wk December 2nd wk October to end November 2nd wk October to 1st November 1st October to 2nd wk November	Beginning to get cold Geese have migrated Lakes and rivers freeze Snow starts to stay in November
atikwaach	Eastern James Bay	September, October, November	Canada and snow geese migrate south Whitefish and lake trout spawn Caribou mate Starts getting cold in October; lakes and rivers freeze High tides, strong winds, and violent storms in coastal areas Porcupine and spruce grouse arrive with the snow Equipment being made for winter hunting and trapping Beaver, marten, mink, and otter trapping starts early November Moose are "nice and fat"
ukiaq	Belcher Islands	November, part December	Days are short; snows most of the time Occasional mild weather and fog Blowing snow; early freezing of sea ice
	Inukjuak Akulivik	Part November, December November, December	Lakes frozen; enough snow to make igloos Sea ice forming in inlets; hunting at floe edge

Season	Location	Months	Characteristics
Fall/Winter *ukiaq*	Coral Harbour Repulse Bay Chesterfield Inlet	November, December	Transitional period from fall to winter Sea ice is forming and safe to walk on; hunting at floe edge Blowing snow; snow stirred up behind landforms by wind Caribou hunting; Arctic char fishing
eh mi ki skak	York Factory Fort Severn	October, November October, November	Waterfowl and birds migrate in October; all have left by October 10 November is "freezing month"; rivers and lakes freeze
Early Winter *mikiskao*	Moose Factory	2nd wk November to end December	Starts to snow
Winter *ukiuq*	Ivujivik Salluit Kangiqsujuaq Lake Harbour Cape Dorset	December, January January, part February December, January, part February Part December, January, February January, February	Cold days and nights; snow builds up steadily; sea ice freezes Land animals have thick fur Travel anywhere: land, lakes, sea ice Seal hunting, ice fishing, fox trapping
	Coral Harbour Repulse Bay Chesterfield Inlet	January, February January, February January, February	Cold Male polar bears come out of their dens Female polar bears on the move
eh po pook	York Factory Fort Severn	December, January, February	December is the month seasonal predictions are made. It is cold but not too cold. January is the "great cold month"—a very dry cold. Ice and snow fall off when tree branches are hit. Days are longer by end of January February is a short, dry, cold month
pipoon	Peawanuck	Mid-December to mid-February	Coldest weather is from mid-January to mid-February First warm spell comes in mid-February
	Kashechewan Fort Albany	December, January, February	High winds; tiny branches fall on the snow Cold starts and stays until first part of February First warm air comes and stays for short while in February
	Moose Factory	January, February, 1st part March	Coldest weather is middle of January
apipuch	Eastern James Bay	December, January, February, March	Cold weather after freeze-up; safe to travel on snow and ice Fur-bearing trapping continues; fox trapping starts when coastal shorelines freeze; beaver trapping finishes end of February Ice fishing with nightlines Beaver mate end of January Days start to lengthen in March; sun is strong; animal fur starts to change Inlanders travel down rivers to goose camps at end of March
ukiuq	Belcher Islands	Part December, January, February	Sunny cold days when land and sea freeze Ice fog due to cold
	Inukjuak	January, February, March	Lake ice gets thicker; snow gets deeper
	Akulivik	January, February	Extremely cold: frost bite can occur on cheeks Days get brighter Good for seal hunting, fishing with nets
"Long Days" *utlutusiq*	Ivujivik Salluit Kangiqsujuaq Lake Harbour Cape Dorset	Part February, March, April Part February, March, April Part February, March, April March, April March	Sun is higher in sky and getting warmer; amount of daylight lengthens each day Good snow; ice still thick Ringed seals born in March; bearded seals in April Seals bask on top of sea ice Ptarmigan start to arrive from the south
	Akulivik	March, April	Clouds are higher, weather is changing; snow thaws occasionally; bearded seals bask on sea ice; polar bears arrive; good season for hunting, fishing with nets
"Towards Spring" *eh kwe ska yak*	York Factory Fort Severn	February, part March	Weather changes from winter to spring People start getting sun- and wind-burned Eagles return in March
makwa pipoon	Peawanuck	Last 3 weeks February	First warm spell comes in mid-February

Season	Location	Months	Characteristics
Early Spring *upingasaq*	Lake Harbour Cape Dorset·	End March, April, part May	Transition from winter to spring; cold air changes to warm Caribou calves born in May
	Coral Harbour	March, April, part May	Transition from winter to spring; end of cold season Female polar bears start to walk around with cubs
	Repulse Bay	March, April, part May	Snow starts thawing Migrating birds, animals start to arrive; insects begin to emerge
	Chesterfield Inlet	March, April, part May	Snow starts to melt; occasional fog Family fishing
	Belcher Islands	March, part April	Days get longer, sun thaws snow-covered areas Snow melts to expose prominent landforms Occasional snow and fog
	Inukjuak	April, part May	Final snow storms; maximum winter snow accumulation Canada geese begin arriving
	Akulivik	May	Snows occasionally; water on sea ice Seals bask on sea ice Canada geese, ducks, and other birds arrive
Spring *upingnaq*	Ivujivik Salluit Kangiqsujuaq Lake Harbour Cape Dorset	May, June May, June May, June Part May, June May, June	Air temperature is warmer every week Old sea ice and snow are melting; lake ice is thin Migrating birds and animals return from south Caribou calves are born in May Birds lay eggs (especially in June); all water animals return
	Coral Harbour Repulse Bay	Part May, June, July Part May, June, July	Snow has melted; birds and ducks arrive Not cold anymore; rains more often than snows; snow is melting Animals arrive; insects emerge
eh see kuk	York Factory Fort Severn	Part March, April, May	Occasional cold and blowing snow Geese return in April; lake ice melts Frogs active in May; rivers may break up at end of May
sikwan	Peawanuck Kashechewan Fort Albany Moose Factory	March, April, 1st part May Part March, April Part March, April Part March, April	Face begins to burn Snow starts to melt before river ice breaks up in mid-April High water levels Slushy
asiikuch	Eastern James Bay	April, May	Bears come out of their dens People go to spring camps to wait for geese, prepare equipment Canada geese start to arrive third week of April Ducks start to arrive beginning of May Spring run-off occurs in May Ice conditions deteriorate; ice crevices form in late spring Snow texture like sand in late spring
upingnaq	Belcher Islands	Part April, May, June, part July	Days are long Warm air, weather at its best; occasional fog Lake and sea ice break up; sea ice prepares to leave
	Inukjuak	Part May, June	Snow starts to melt; rivers start to flow Natural holes form in lake ice; water on top of sea ice
	Akulivik	June	Seals moult and bask on top of sea ice People jig or use nets for fish Spring camping All ducks and birds have arrived
Between Spring/Summer *minoskamin*	Peawanuck Kashechewan Fort Albany Moose Factory	1st part May to 1st part June May to 3rd wk June May to 3rd wk June May	Snow and ice melt; ice breaks up in rivers and lakes Coastal sea ice breaks up third week of June in Kashechewan and Fort Albany areas Grass and leaves turn green

Season	Location	Months	Characteristics
Early Summer *upingalaq*	Ivujivik Salluit Kangiqsujuaq Lake Harbour	July Part June, part July June July	Long days, short nights Sea ice melts; drifts away from mainland No snow Wildlife have arrived for summer Birds and ducks nest; eggs from large birds now available Arctic char migrate to seawater
	Akulivik	July	Lake and sea ice are gone Plants and berries grow Arctic char are in the seawater Mosquitoes and house flies are present
Summer *aujaq*	Ivujivik Salluit Kangiqsujuaq Lake Harbour Cape Dorset	August Part July, August July, August August, part September July, August	Warmer weather; older winter ice gone Land vegetation grows: e.g., crowberries, blueberries Eggs and plants are edible Lots of mosquitoes Land starts changing colour in August Walrus are on the move in August Nights are longer
	Coral Harbour Repulse Bay Chesterfield Inlet	August August June, July, August	Arctic char migrate upstream to lakes Dry season; little rain Weather not too cold; mosquitoes present; birds can be heard
eh nee pik	York Factory Fort Severn	June, July, part August	Open-water season after ice breaks up and leaves Birds lay eggs in June Sturgeon spawn when leaves are the size of beaver ears Geese and ducks moult in July, are ready to fly in August
nipin	Peawanuck Kashechewan Fort Albany Moose Factory	Mid-June, July, 1st August End June, July, Aug., 1st part Sept. End June, July, Aug., 1st part Sept. June, July, August	Open water in rivers, lakes, and the bay Mid-summer occurs the middle of July
aniipich	Eastern James Bay	June, July, August	Open-water season Rivers and lakes not frozen Snow geese begin migrating north in early June Caribou and moose get parasites and lose a lot of weight Fishing only; no hunting and trapping Fish start going upstream in mid-August
aujaq	Belcher Islands	Part July, August	Sun is warm; fog, rain, and occasional thunderstorms Plants growing Sea waves build up
	Inukjuak	July, August	Lots of mosquitoes in mid-summer Arctic char are in the sea
	Akulivik	August, September	Sea waves build up Rains more often Land plants turn reddish colour Ducks and birds return south Arctic char migrate upriver from sea

Appendix C: Environmental Indicators

Environmental Condition	Indicator	Geographical Reference
Bad Weather • with rain or wind • for two to three days • later in the day • same day or next • next day • in the spring or early summer • wind storms–spring/early summer • coming • coming–spring	Wildlife aren't around Birds travel in flocks Currents are mixed up and change directions rapidly Seawater comes up over the top of ice in winter High tides Threatening-looking clouds to the left or right of the sun at daybreak Sand particles in water Sky is red at sunrise Currents are active towards the full moon Small cloud just above the daylight when sun starts to rise Sun is a reddish colour in early morning Caribou or seals shake their heads On calm days, dogs stay inside igloo porch and start to shake their bodies or roll over to clean themselves for no real reason In winter, halo appears around sun or moon just before it sets Stars called "tuktuyuit" and "sakiasiak" blink on a clear night Dark, thick clouds Canada geese fly south during their spring migration High waves start coming in on a calm day Direction of strong winds is based on direction of rolling waves Animals aren't around Geese migrating north start flying south	Hudson Strait Eastern Hudson Bay Western Hudson Bay Eastern Hudson Bay Hudson Strait Eastern Hudson Bay Hudson Strait Eastern Hudson Bay Hudson Strait Hudson Strait
Very Bad Weather	Geese do not move	Hudson Strait
Not So Good Weather • same day • next day	Moon has a light colour just before it sets West wind; eastern sky isn't necessarily red Thin layer of clouds gets dark in places Sun is bright red as it sets Echoes travel for miles	Eastern Hudson Bay
Stormy Weather • for a few days • unusually long • doesn't get better • not long • long and windy	Clouds seem to be moving into the wind Winds shift more than once in short time Winds keep changing without slowing down Clouds are coming with the wind A couple of thick layers of clouds	Hudson Strait
Storm • same day • coming • building up • big storm coming • snow storm	No animals anywhere on a nice day Haze out in the bay Birds gather in large numbers; animals move in same direction Feather-like clouds appear at low tide; eastern sky is red at sunrise Cirro-cumulus clouds appear and cover a clear, blue sky	Hudson Strait Eastern James Bay Hudson Strait Eastern Hudson Bay Hudson Strait
Better Weather • next day • may even turn calm • coming	Flat clouds Reddish colour sun rays in evening Halo changes from a yellowish to rainbow colour in stormy weather Large white clouds on a windy day Clouds are not in layers Land or island mirage appears on horizon Horned larks, Lapland longspurs, and snow buntings become active Wind slows down on a windy day Winds blow continuously from one direction Animals start moving around in bad weather Geese fly high even on windy days	Hudson Strait Hudson Strait
Good Weather • brings	Rainbow appears around the sun Big fluffy clouds Moon stands straight up Sky is red at sunset Clean sea ice (after break-up)	Hudson Strait Eastern Hudson Bay Western Hudson Bay Eastern Hudson Bay
Clear Weather	Skies clear up over the bay after being cloudy for a few days	Western Hudson Bay

Environmental Condition	Indicator	Geographical Reference
Blue Sky • coming • not staying	Appears on northwestern horizon during a thick, cloudy day Appears from nowhere and passes by	Eastern Hudson Bay
Cold Weather • part of the day • for four or five days • coming • extremely cold	Rainbow on both sides of the sun in morning Woodpecker's beak moves fast Halo around the sun appears close to the sun Bright halo above the sun either in morning or in evening Sun has bright spots and a lighter halo around it Grouse are fat Bright northern lights cover entire sky	Eastern Hudson Bay Western Hudson Bay Western James Bay Eastern James Bay Western Hudson Bay
Warmer Weather • for almost a week • for only short time • more warm weather during week • within hours, for about 3 days	Large halo appears around the sun or moon (in either summer or winter) Halo around the sun is in close proximity to the sun Small black flies fall on the snow Northern lights are reddish-orange on their southern side	Eastern Hudson Bay Western James Bay Western Hudson Bay
Mild or Warm Weather • might change–for half day only • for part of the day–afternoon only • next day	Thick reddish cloud in winter Halo is far from the sun Northern lights move in one direction Woodpecker's beak moves slowly Chickadees appear suddenly during cold day	Hudson Strait Western Hudson Bay
Very Mild Weather	Quick lightning flash	Hudson Strait
Calm	Northern lights do not move	Western Hudson Bay
Wind Direction • will blow mostly from southeast • indicators for next day	Sun is reddish colour Cirrus clouds with "hooks" Northern lights Direction of falling stars	Eastern Hudson Bay Western James Bay
Windy • with rough water • gusts	Northern lights move east to west Campstove makes whistling sound Sun goes dark Red-throated loon calls out Sun becomes hazy on calm day in summer	Western Hudson Bay Northwestern Hudson Bay Western Hudson Bay Northwestern Hudson Bay
Strong Winds or Storm	Halo around the sun	Eastern James Bay
Strong Winds • coming • may come from any direction • during the day • won't slow down • will slow down • for two to three days	Glowing red sun Lots of northern lights in a clear sky Dark cloud appears from nowhere and disappears again Long, thin clouds above other clouds in a mostly blue sky Small birds fly in large groups Bottom of moon is light-coloured early in morning Clouds move counter-clockwise Winds are blowing clockwise Winds change directions quickly without settling down	Hudson Strait Eastern Hudson Bay Hudson Strait Eastern Hudson Bay
Low Pressure System	Geese fly low	Hudson Strait
Tides • high • very big	Moon is bigger Full moon	Western Hudson Bay
Rain • later same day or next day	Beavers shake their heads Small black flies come every day Dark clouds in evening Loon cries and flies off in evening Call of the red-throated loon	Eastern James Bay Western James Bay Western Hudson Bay Hudson Strait

Environmental Condition	Indicator	Geographical Reference
Snow • rest of the month • next day • falling snow, blowing snow • falling snow • next day • snowfall or will turn very foggy	First or third quarter moon is upright Cracking ice makes large booming sounds Half moon is leaning to one side Owls call at night Large, thick, white, oval clouds in winter Scattered clouds Dark clouds appear with white, round clouds as the sun is about to set on a nice calm day Long, smooth ice fog shows up	Eastern Hudson Bay Western Hudson Bay Eastern Hudson Bay Western Hudson Bay Hudson Strait Eastern Hudson Bay
Blizzards	Rainbow appears around the moon	Hudson Strait
Ice • freshwater ice will be slushy	Air makes a "bubbly" sound in the ice during night and day in winter	Western Hudson Bay
Sea-ice Safety • floe-edge ice will not break away • ice is safe	Ice fog in mountains and lower valleys Ice fog is down to the ground	Hudson Strait
Seasonal Changes • changing from cold to warmer • thin layer of ice on top of snow will not freeze anymore • snowmelt will begin and continue • beluga whales will be coming • sea gulls will lay eggs • Arctic char will return from seawater	Particular animals coming and going Rotation of big dipper When snow buntings and Lapland longspurs arrive When rough-legged hawks start to arrive (spring) When falcons arrive (past) When common and red-throated loons start to arrive When wet snow begins to occur When snow geese, sandpipers, and shorebirds start migrating south	Hudson Strait Western Hudson Bay Hudson Strait
Fall • nice weather • coming • early snowfall	High tides Particular sound of a woodpecker Fish going upriver Rabbit paws turn white early	Eastern Hudson Bay Western James Bay Hudson Strait Western James Bay
Winter • will be early • will be warm or cold • warm weather • cold or rough winter • long winter • less cold • Christmas	Grass turns yellow in September Type of cracking sound in the trees at night in the first frosty weather Thunder in late fall Foggy in fall Rabbit paws change to white in October instead of November Fall skies are clear Beaver or moose give birth to small offspring Big dipper turns its tail to the north Big dipper is straight up at sunrise	Western James Bay Western Hudson Bay Western James Bay Western Hudson Bay Western James Bay Western Hudson Bay
Spring • coming • beginning • early • long • difficult	Thick-billed murres arrive Begin to see walrus (past) Black bear leaves den in early April A particular underwater lake and river plant is about 2″ [50 mm] long Black bear walks out in April South wind during April full moon Pussy willows sprout in February Big dipper is directly overhead by mid-December, January Groundhog comes out February 2 Evening star is high at dawn Groundhog doesn't come out February 2	Hudson Strait Western James Bay Western James Bay Western Hudson Bay Western James Bay Western Hudson Bay Western Hudson Bay
Summer • early • warm weather • hot	Evening star is low at dawn Bright red sunset Thunder in early spring	Western Hudson Bay Western James Bay Western Hudson Bay

Environmental Condition	Indicator	Geographical Reference
Sea Mammals • coming	Eider ducks start coming	Cape Dorset
Moose • close by	Two stars on the north and south side of the moon	Western James Bay
Caribou • coming or increasing in number	Influx of wolves when only a few caribou	Western Hudson Bay
Birds • fly back out	Fly in during a frost	Northwestern Hudson Bay

Animal Populations
• generally high
  • fox—high
  • geese—high
  • geese—low
	Lots of thunder and lightning in summer
	Sudden population explosion in mice during summer
	Snow birds come first, and from the east
	Snow birds come from west
		Western Hudson Bay
		Western Hudson Bay

Appendix D: Environmental Changes in Sturgeon, Snow Goose, Canada Goose, Beluga Whale, and Polar Bear

Sturgeon

Sturgeon are extremely sensitive to water-quality changes, and traditionally great care was taken not to disturb them. In eastern James Bay, no one was allowed to scoop water in *sturgeon places* with anything that had been used for cooking. Sturgeon are also sensitive to other water disturbances such as run-off after a heavy rain, wind direction, thunderstorms, rusty water, and flooded vegetation.

The cleanest fish in the water is sturgeon. You throw something into the water, like different kinds of fish blood, they will move away from there. Even when you spear them, if blood is there when they're spawning, they'll move away. That's how clean they are.

Mary Shanoush, Moose Factory

In the past, Cree caught sturgeon all along La Grande River and depended on it for sustenance. Today, there are no sturgeon in La Grande River because the

sturgeon is very, very aware of the water system. It's very sensitive to water change, and will go further inland to where the waters are not affected. It will find rivers where there is no change.

William Fireman, Chisasibi

The sturgeon disappeared from their original habitat at LG-2 and LG-3 and were not found again until the summer of 1992, when they were located as far inland as they could travel:

... very far from their original habitat.... We found the spawning area, and the sturgeon there are very healthy. They are not like the other fish, which are not even fit to eat. This is because the sturgeon is a very strong survivor, and a very strong swimmer, even in a strong current.

William Fireman, Chisasibi

Sturgeon in the Sakami River area (eastern James Bay) were abundant and very healthy in the 1930s and 1940s; in the 1990s they are fewer in number and are less healthy. Water levels have risen and there are no longer rapids at the Sakami's source where sturgeon and other fish used to spawn:

All this area downstream from the rapids, and including all of Sakami, was inhabited by sturgeon. Since diversion of the Eastmain River, the water level rises at Sakami and the fish are not as good as they were before the flooding.

John Matches, Wemindji

In southern James Bay, sturgeon on the Abitibi and Mattagami rivers get caught below the dam gates and die in small ponds from lack of oxygen when water levels go down. As well, some Cree have observed changes in the physical characteristics of the sturgeon:

I find sturgeon in the Harrikanaw River very different. The people I share them with find the meat is heavier and stronger tasting. The meat goes soft [within] a day or even half a day. The body seems to lose form. It starts to look like it has only been a head. The sturgeon look like that since they started building dams. They are gradually losing their body, [and] they're not healthy like the fish you find in other areas where there is no dam close by. [There's] also the paper mill.

Jimmy Small, Moose Factory

In western Hudson Bay, when the Jenpeg dam was constructed, sturgeon at Norway House in the Nelson River system went downstream; when the Kelsey dam was constructed, the sturgeon went farther downstream. Because dam gates prevent them from moving back upriver, a lot of sturgeon are now concentrated below the Limestone dam. Construction of the proposed Conawapa dam would push the sturgeon even farther downstream and into saline waters. York Factory Cree question whether the sturgeon would survive.

Snow goose

Eastern James Bay coastal Cree relate that, long ago, the snow geese flew in large flocks during spring migration. Beginning in May, one flock would land, feed, and leave and another flock would come right after. This would continue until the 10th of June. So many flocks were coming in that people north of

Figure D-1: Changes in Snow Goose Flyways

Source: Hudson Bay Programme, *Traditional Ecological Knowledge of Environmental Changes in Hudson and James Bays, Part I.* (Ottawa: HBP, 1995), 50.

Chisasibi thought there was not enough space for them to land. Today, both spring and fall coastal migrations have declined and although some geese still migrate along the eastern James Bay coast, most now either fly inland along the mountains of mid-northern Quebec and up through Caniapiscau, or cross over to or from the west side of James Bay passing into or from Hudson Bay past Cape Jones (figure D-1).

In marked contrast to the few snow geese that arrived in spring or fall for many years, snow geese have recently been passing through Ivujivik by the thousands over a one-month period of non-stop flying. Inuit attribute the increase to new travel routes and the role of wind in determining how snow geese migrate north or south.[1]

The Quebec mainland bordering the Hudson Strait is the last staging area for snow geese crossing over the strait to Baffin Island and the moulting area for those unable to make the crossing. The moulting geese have become so many that, *sometimes, the side of land* [looks] *as if it is sliding sideways because of the number of geese moving in the same direction at the same time.*

More snow geese now enter the western side of James Bay from the west and then travel up the coast to nest and moult in the Cape Henrietta Maria area. Twenty years ago the Cape Henrietta snow geese would fly inland to feed after nesting and moulting. Once their condition improved, they would resume flying up the southwestern coast of Hudson Bay, stopping and feeding along the way until their fall migration. At that time, they would turn around and migrate south along the coastal route, leaving the region through Hannah Bay. Since the 1980s, however, fewer snow geese migrate south following the coast. Instead, earlier in the season, they fly inland from the James Bay coast to spend more time feeding until their fall migration west begins.

In spring, snow geese are reported flying from the west to arrive the 12th of May in Fort Severn. Some stay, but by the 26th of June most have migrated farther north to nest and moult. Since 1985 the Fort Severn and York Factory snow geese also have been leaving earlier in the fall and flying to the west instead of south. The first group starts leaving about the first week of September and all are gone by the 10th of October.

The snow geese follow the same routes along the northwestern Hudson Bay coast during their spring and fall migrations. Large nesting areas are found in the Arviat area and the southern part of Southampton Island.

Canada goose

Canada geese usually arrive and leave earlier than snow geese and nest farther south than snow geese.

Like snow geese, Canada geese have shifted from the eastern James Bay coast to inland routes, which they now follow to Hudson Strait. Unlike snow geese, they appear to fly more directly over La Grande reservoir. Some Canada geese still fly along the coast, but farther offshore (figure D-2).

There are two spring migrations of Canada geese on the eastern side of the basin. Inuit in Baffin Island report that mating adult Canada geese arrive first; younger geese, leaner than the adults, come later for moulting and do not nest.

Belcher Islands Inuit and eastern James Bay Cree also see a second migration of Canada geese. They are greater Canada geese that fly in only to moult. In eastern James Bay, the greater Canada geese used to fly inland to moult in the marshes before going down to the rivers when their young started to fly. In recent years, Cree at Roggan River and in areas south of Wemindji and Waskaganish have started seeing large flocks flying low in June, following the tree line of the bay. These geese stop their migration wherever they land, because they have already started moulting and they are unable to fly any farther. They seem not to be as naturally wild as the earlier arrivals; because of their late arrival and because they are more aggressive, both the Cree and Inuit believe they arrive from urban areas.

In western Hudson Bay, Cree have distinct names for the three flocks of Canada geese—nesting, mid-size, and large flocks—based on their behaviour, not their appearance. The nesting geese come into the Peawanuck area in pairs about the 20th of April, and the larger flocks start arriving about the 10th of May from either the south or the west, depending on the weather.

York Factory hunters have noticed a change in the autumn migration routes of Canada geese. In the past they would follow the coastal route, but now arrive from the bay, land at Marsh Point, then head west.

Both Inuit and Cree maintain that wind is an important factor in determining the actual flyways of Canada geese. In the Inukjuak area, for example, the geese

Figure D-2: Changes in Canada Goose Flyways

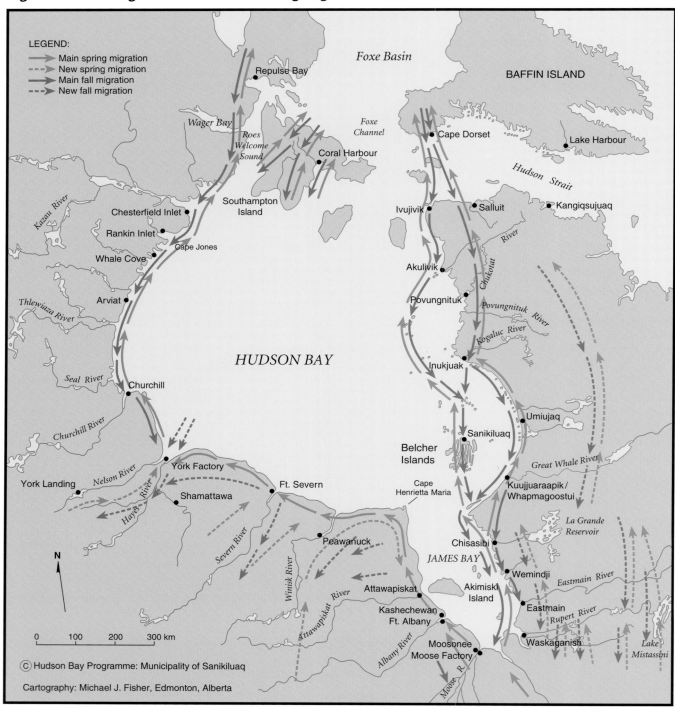

Source: Hudson Bay Programme, *Traditional Ecological Knowledge of Environmental Changes in Hudson and James Bays, Part I.* (Ottawa: HBP, 1995), 52.

typically fly in from Umiujaq during the spring migration; however, if there is a continuous north wind they will take an inland flyway rather than migrate past Inukjuak.

Beluga whale

Three populations of beluga whale use Hudson Bay: eastern Hudson Bay beluga migrate into the bay along the southern shoreline of Hudson Strait; southwestern Hudson Bay-James Bay beluga over-winter; and northwestern Hudson Bay beluga migrate into the area along the northern shoreline of Hudson Strait (figure D-3).

Most eastern Hudson Bay beluga migrate past Ivujivik and into Hudson Strait from Hudson Bay in September and October. It is believed the last ones leaving the bay remain all winter in Hudson Strait. Northwestern Hudson Bay beluga leave the Southampton Island area, migrating past Cape Dorset in October, to winter near Lake Harbour. In southern James Bay, beluga are still feeding in Moose Factory and Hannah Bay in October.

Although large numbers of beluga migrate northward in September and October from their summer feeding areas, there is evidence that a relatively large population winters in the bay. This over-wintering should not be confused with occasional entrapments of beluga throughout the bay. It appears to be one regular wintering population or more, and may be a "stock" discrete from the belugas leaving Hudson Bay to winter in Hudson Strait or elsewhere.

Beluga continue to be sighted throughout the winter at the floe edge southwest and west of the Belcher Islands and in eastern James Bay (Chisasibi), southeastern Hudson Bay, and southwestern Hudson Bay (Peawanuck). They are also sighted at the floe edge in northwestern Hudson Bay (Southampton Island and Repulse Bay), northeastern Hudson Bay (Ivujivik area), and eastern Hudson Bay (Akulivik and Inukjuak). Beluga breathing holes in winter are reported in all areas where currents keep the ice thin and, in southwestern Hudson Bay, whale breathing is heard in winter from under ice-pressure ridges.

In spring (May and June), beluga migrate west along the shorelines of Hudson Strait and enter Hudson Bay; they are fat during this season and are reported "very fat" by July.[2] Although the end of June is the earliest that sea-ice conditions allow beluga to enter Hudson

Bay from Hudson Strait, some from the wintering population in Hudson Bay are seen some months earlier in James Bay and southern Hudson Bay. Beluga appear in April in newly opened sea-ice cracks north of the Belcher Islands and near the Sleeper Islands. They are also seen in the Southampton Island and Repulse Bay areas at about the same time. They travel through the Charlton Island area in southwestern James Bay as soon as there is open water in spring (late March and April), and are first sighted immediately after break-up and as soon as the water opens in late May at Moose Factory and Attawapiskat. Likewise, when the ice breaks up in late May-early June, they start coming into the rivers of southwestern Hudson Bay.

Inuit report that the beluga have abandoned some traditional areas, especially near Inukjuak and Salluit. In the Inukjuak area, whales move away when boats approach to within three or four kilometres, and in Salluit beluga appear to react to boats up to eight kilometres distant. Certain places formerly frequented by beluga in the Inukjuak area where summer boat traffic is particularly heavy (e.g., Nauliqavik and Kutaaq) no longer have beluga. They visit the Great Whale River later in the season, after the shipping traffic has subsided.

Consensus among Inuit hunters is that beluga will always move to areas where food is abundant and it is peaceful. Arctic cod, a principal food of beluga, has become scarce in the Repulse Bay area and the beluga are now reported to be more abundant in the Hall Beach and Igloolik areas to the north. Eastern Hudson Bay beluga have moved to travel in currents farther offshore. Large numbers of beluga are now reported in the southwestern Hudson Bay region, where whitefish are plentiful and beluga-hunting for food for dog teams no longer occurs. In James Bay, beluga seek the whitefish. Other beluga foods reported from Hudson Bay include Arctic cod and char (Chesterfield and Repulse Bay); capelin (Churchill); sculpins (Inukjuak); Arctic cod, sculpins, crustacea, and sea cucumbers (Kuujjuaraapik).

Beluga often swim into strong currents and enter certain rivers—in the Inukjuak area (July), Chisasibi (June and July), Nottaway River (July), Rupert River (August), Moose River (August), Peawanuck (September)—to feed. As well, the annual moult takes place in rivers. Beluga enter suitable rivers, where they roll on the sandy bottom or against sandbars to assist the

Figure D-3: Beluga Whale Distribution in Hudson and James Bays

LEGEND:
- Spring migration
- Fall migration
- Spring locations
- Winter locations

Foxe Basin

BAFFIN ISLAND

Repulse Bay

Wager Bay

Foxe Channel

Cape Dorset

Lake Harbour

Roes Welcome Sound

Southampton Island

Coral Harbour

Hudson Strait

Kazan River

Chesterfield Inlet

Ivujivik

Salluit

Kangiqsujuaq

Rankin Inlet

Cape Jones

Whale Cove

Akulivik

Chukotat River

Thlewiaza River

Arviat

Povungnituk

Povungnituk River

Kogaluc River

Inukjuak

HUDSON BAY

Seal River

Churchill

Umiujaq

Churchill River

Sanikiluaq

Belcher Islands

Great Whale River

York Factory

York Landing

Nelson River

Hayes River

Ft. Severn

Cape Henrietta Maria

Kuujjuaraapik / Whapmagoostui

Shamattawa

La Grande Reservoir

Chisasibi

Peawanuck

JAMES BAY

Wemindji

Eastmain River

Winisk River

Severn River

Attawapiskat River

Attawapiskat

Akimiski Island

Eastmain

Kashechewan

Ft. Albany

Rupert River

Waskaganish

Lake Mistassini

Albany River

Moosonee

Moose Factory

Moose R.

N

0   100   200   300 km

© Hudson Bay Programme: Municipality of Sanikiluaq

Cartography: Michael J. Fisher, Edmonton, Alberta

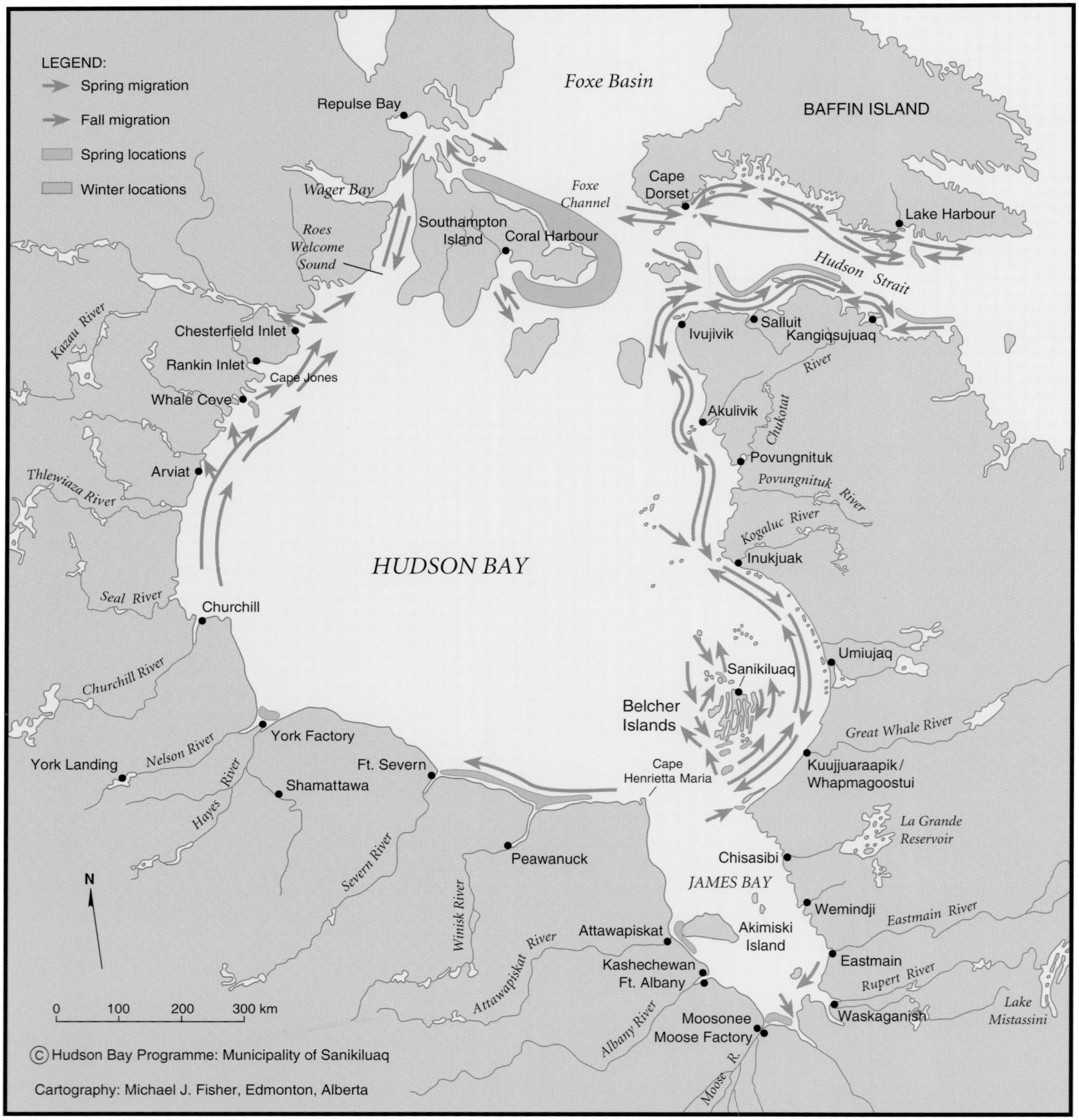

Source: Hudson Bay Programme, *Traditional Ecological Knowledge of Environmental Changes in Hudson and James Bays, Part I.* (Ottawa: HBP, 1995), 54.

moulting process. Boat traffic has caused beluga to abandon some former moulting sites in the Great Whale, Kutaaq, and Nauliqavik rivers. The Little Whale River, Nastapoka River, and Richmond Gulf areas have become important moulting sites. There are no rivers suitable for moulting on the Belcher Islands; however, beluga may rub against sea ice to assist the moult.

The beluga breeding season is reported to be variable. In the Repulse Bay area, newborn beluga are observed at any time of the year, whereas in Hudson Bay newborns are reported principally in July. Also, in Hudson Bay, female beluga have either a fetus or an accompanying newborn each spring, and each female accompanied by a yearling calf—identified by colour and size—usually carries a fetus. (By their third year, although grey in colour, the young are nearly the same size as the adult female.) These occurrences indicate that an annual calving takes place. On the few occasions that females are not accompanied by a calf, it is believed the calf has been lost.

The only areas identified as discrete calving areas for beluga are found in the Repulse Bay-Frozen Strait area and the area northwest of Iqaluit. Belugas are known to give birth while they are moving and the actual birthing process averages three days.

Polar bears

In late summer, *sikujuaniq*[3] from Hudson Bay carries lots of polar bears past Kangiqsujuaq; however, it is not known where these bears originate (figure D-4). Few now come to the Ivujivik area, and Kangiqsujuaq residents report that, during winter, they have not seen polar bears in their area for a long time. Inuit in Cape Dorset report few polar bears in their area, although the number varies from year to year and more are present when the young seals are born.

Polar bears are most populous during summer in Southampton Island and are seen occasionally in the Arviat-Whale Cove-Chesterfield Inlet coastal areas at that time. They are most numerous in the Chesterfield Inlet area in September, and a number are present in the Arviat area between September and December. Although some stay for denning, most leave the Arviat and Whale Cove areas as soon as the sea ice begins to form in December.

In the Akulivik area, polar bears arrive in December, when strong winds blow from the northwest during the early freezing of sea ice. More are in the area after ice has formed between the islands in February. They also come to the Inukjuak, Belcher Islands, and Long Island areas as soon as the sea ice starts forming in December.

Polar bears are rarely seen in the Umiujaq area during winter because they spend most of their time at the distant floe edge, which in the early 1990s extended from west of Long Island along the west side of Belcher-Split-Sleeper islands all the way to Inukjuak.

Although most polar bears leave once the pack ice starts moving out of eastern Hudson Bay, some remain year-round; sightings are reported near Inukjuak in August, the Umiujaq near-shore islands, the Kuujjuaraapik coastal and near-shore island area, and offshore islands in the Belcher Islands archipelago. Reports from Akulivik confirm that polar bears stop in that area during the mid-summer months. The bears also summer in Long Island and northeastern James Bay, where they are occasionally seen inland, and in the North Twin Island area.

There are more polar bears in southwestern Hudson Bay than in northwestern James Bay. They are sighted in the Attawapiskat area but not in the Moose Factory, Fort Albany, or Kashechewan areas. In the Fort Severn and York Factory areas, they are seen mostly during the fall.

Polar bears in northwestern James Bay and southwestern Hudson Bay stay on the sea ice until it begins to move offshore and melt in July or August. The females and yearling cubs come ashore first and spend time along the shore before travelling about 80 kilometres inland. The males usually leave the ice in August and live along the shoreline until it becomes slushy with early winter ice.

The females return to the coast in October to leave their yearling cubs at the shoreline to mix with the older males while the females go back inland to den.[4] Later in October, when seals move away from the slushy ice, the polar bear yearlings follow the adult males inland as far as the tree line, where they stay until the sea ice begins to thicken. After returning to the shore, they congregate in groups of up to 20 until the ice is firm enough to support their weight; then they begin to travel to the floe edge.

In August, the embryos are only small "blisters" on the uterine walls. At birth, in approximately the third week of December in western and southwestern Hudson Bay, the cubs are about the size of squirrels. The

Figure D-4: Polar Bear Seasonal Activity in Selected Areas of Hudson Bay

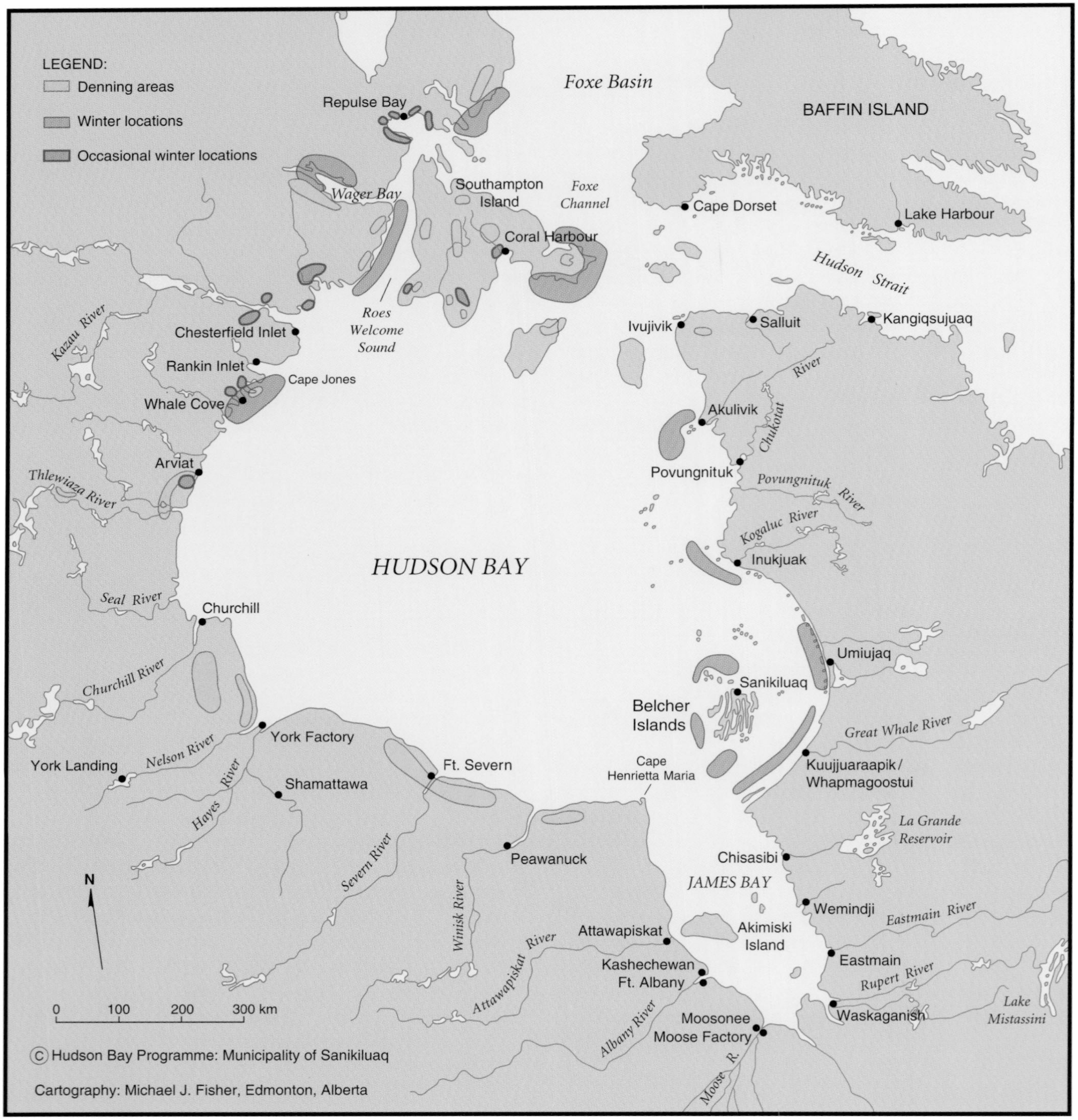

LEGEND:
- Denning areas
- Winter locations
- Occasional winter locations

Foxe Basin

BAFFIN ISLAND

Repulse Bay

Wager Bay

Southampton Island

Foxe Channel

Cape Dorset

Lake Harbour

Coral Harbour

Hudson Strait

Roes Welcome Sound

Kazau River

Chesterfield Inlet

Ivujivik

Salluit

Kangiqsujuaq

Rankin Inlet

Cape Jones

Whale Cove

Akulivik

Chukotat River

Arviat

Povungnituk

Povungnituk River

Thlewiaza River

Kogaluc River

Inukjuak

HUDSON BAY

Seal River

Churchill

Umiujaq

Churchill River

Sanikiluaq

Belcher Islands

Great Whale River

York Factory

Ft. Severn

Cape Henrietta Maria

Kuujjuaraapik / Whapmagoostui

York Landing

Nelson River

Hayes River

Shamattawa

La Grande Reservoir

Peawanuck

Severn River

Chisasibi

JAMES BAY

Wemindji

Eastmain River

N

Winisk River

Attawapiskat River

Attawapiskat

Akimiski Island

Eastmain

0   100   200   300 km

Kashechewan
Ft. Albany

Albany River

Rupert River

Waskaganish

Lake Mistassini

© Hudson Bay Programme: Municipality of Sanikiluaq

Moosonee
Moose Factory

Moose R.

Cartography: Michael J. Fisher, Edmonton, Alberta

Source: *Hudson Bay Programme, Traditional Ecological Knowledge Management Systems Study, 1992–1995.*

mothers do not eat anything while denning and resume eating only after returning to the bay with newborn cubs. Trappers usually see the females travelling to the coast with newborns by mid-March.[5] A female polar bear usually has two cubs; however, recently in southwestern Hudson Bay, adult females have been noticed returning from denning with three or four cubs. Reproduction rates may be increasing in response to a reduced demand for meat for dog teams and the introduction of hunting quotas in the 1960s.

At the bay, the females travel with their cubs to the floe edge (about eight kilometres offshore), where they make a den. They spend the next six months training their cubs and will leave them in the den while going out into the open water to hunt.

In the Chesterfield Inlet area, the number of bears has increased since 1988. There are also more bears in Arviat, where they sometimes walk between the houses in September. Polar bear numbers have been increasing in the Repulse Bay area since the 1940s and 1950s; in 1992-93, polar bears were so numerous in Southampton Island that the quota of 65 was filled in three days. Northwestern Hudson Bay Inuit predict increasing danger for humans in camps if quotas are reduced from their pre-1992 levels.

Weakening currents and more extensive ice cover in eastern Hudson Bay are thought to be why polar bears are no longer seen in the Ivujivik area during mid-winter. The expanded ice cover increases the winter range of polar bears, so they are spending more time on the sea ice west of Inukjuak than at the mouth of Hudson Strait.

The number of polar bears has been increasing, particularly since the 1960s, in the Akulivik, Inukjuak, and Belcher Islands areas. Although archaeological evidence establishes that polar bears once inhabited Cape Smith Island, there were none in the Akulivik area in the 1930s and 1940s. Belcher Islands Inuit recall few polar bears in the offshore islands of eastern Hudson Bay 40 to 50 years ago. Similarly, Inukjuak representatives report that polar bears started to appear *not too long ago*. Inuit think polar bears may be shifting to eastern Hudson Bay because of the abundance of ringed seals, an expanding floe edge, and polar bear hunting quotas unchanged since the 1970s.

In the Fort Severn area, polar bear populations are relatively stable; however, in the northwestern James Bay-southwestern Hudson Bay area populations are increasing. Population fluctuations over time are known to be natural.

Polar bears are opportunists whose diet includes ringed seal, bearded seal, walrus, beluga whale, lemming, cached caribou, Arctic char, eider duck, birds' eggs, crowberries, Greenland lousewort, seaweed, grass, soil, plastic bags, and engine oil. Their preference is seal fat, and when they are going to eat mostly fat they first eat soil or seaweed to help keep the fat oil in their stomachs longer. They are known to forage dump-sites and hunting camps, particularly in the western and northwestern areas of Hudson Bay. At one time, meat stored up to 160 kilometres from Repulse Bay was safe, but now bears are getting into the caches. Those that have become used to foraging in garbage dumps are reported to have lost their natural hunting ability.

While polar bears are inland near Fort Severn and York Factory during the summer, they eat the same type of grass—it grows in beaver dams and is about 45 centimetres tall—that muskrat eat. They have also acquired an appetite for engine oil, and they forage hunting camps for oil left unattended. Inuit hunters in the Whale Cove and Repulse Bay areas will no longer make incisions into polar bear stomachs because if the snowmobile oil has resided in the stomach very long it blackens the contents and emits a strong, offensive smell.

York Factory residents report that polar bears in their area are skinny and they identify the *poor ones* seen in late fall by their scratching behaviour and deep cuts. In spring 1991, ten young dogs died from eating the flesh of a polar bear with worms.

Some of the polar bears approaching Whale Cove and Chesterfield Inlet in the fall are also very lean, and Inuit from Southampton Island report that bears appeared leaner and more aggressive in 1993 than in 1992.

In eastern Hudson Bay, only the polar bears that have been marked, tattooed, collared, tagged, and tranquillized by wildlife research teams are reported in poor shape. In southwestern Hudson Bay, residents could not assess body condition because they no longer hunt polar bears regularly.

Throughout Hudson Bay, polar bears have lost their fear of humans and dogs. In western and northwestern Hudson Bay they are becoming increasingly aggressive and more dependent on foraging dump-sites, camp sites, and meat caches.

Notes

1. The Cree also observe geese moving according to the winds and report that additional snow geese fly into southwestern Hudson Bay from the northeast in the fall. At the time of their arrival, they will fly into James Bay if there is a strong north wind.

2. The beluga going into eastern Hudson Bay wait in the Ivujivik area until the sea ice is gone. The males arrive first and wait for the females; then they enter eastern Hudson Bay together after the sea ice has broken up.

3. *Sikujuaniq* is dirty, old-looking pack ice that doesn't melt away in the early summer season.

4. In southwestern Hudson Bay, female polar bears travel 30 to 120 kilometres inland to deliver their cubs.

5. Female polar bears typically travel in a straight direction through the trees and muskeg when they go inland to den. When they go back to the coast with newborns they go through areas where the young cubs can travel—usually a route that follows the hard-packed snow.

Appendix E: Summary Information on Geese

Snow Goose Summary Information					
Community/ Region	**Species/ Season**	**Arrive**	**Leave**	**Nest, Moult, Feed, or Pass Through**	**Comments**
Moose Factory	Fall	September 20	End of October	Feeding	Moose Factory is the last staging area for snow geese migrating south. In the past 50 years they are fewer in number and their stay is shorter as a result of habitat changes. Willows, brush, and grass have started growing in primary feeding areas; geese tend to fly inland to eat during the day, and then return to the coast in the evening. Very few snow geese have been seen in the Moose Factory/ Hannah Bay area the past few years; numbers were especially low in the fall of 1993.
Western James Bay	Spring, Fall	Early May	September	Nesting and moulting	Snow geese usually arrive from the west during the first week of May. Cape Henrietta Maria is their last staging area before flying out of James Bay to cross Hudson Bay. Some stay in the area for about a month, then continue their spring migration; others nest and moult in the Cape Henrietta Maria area until their food supply is depleted, then move out of the area in search of more food. In the past, the snow geese nesting at Cape Henrietta Maria started flying southwards when the first cold weather arrived in September. In the last 20 years, however, they leave Cape Henrietta Maria by August 20th and fly into the western coastal area of James Bay. Some stay in the Attawapiskat River area until their fall migration; others feed only for a short while there, then fly north again. Snow geese remaining in the area are the first to leave the coastal region in the fall, flying about 150 kilometres inland. They don't return. The other geese that have flown north stop to eat in areas along the coast until the first cold, frosty weather arrives in September. At that time, they start their southward migration by flying inland, where they stay in the Attawapiskat-Ekwani-Swan River areas until the next cold weather comes in October. Cree started noticing the snow geese migrating west instead of south in about 1984.
Peawanuck	Fall (past)	End of August	Mid-October	Feeding	Fifty years ago, snow geese left in mid-October, after the Canada geese, and flew straight south. The small, weaker ones were the last to leave.
	(present)	Mid-August, first week of September	Early September		Today, there are usually many snow geese at Winisk River mouth in the last week of August and first week of September. Those that fly in from Cape Henrietta Maria fly north during the last two weeks of August, returning during the first week of September with those that had migrated farther north. They do not stay long before flying west in early September. Residents of Big Trout Lake and Webequie notice snow geese have started coming into their muskeg areas about 320 kilometres inland. They have been flying west in noticeable numbers since 1988.
	Fall	September	October	Feeding, passing through	Snow geese from the Arctic start arriving the end of September. They feed in marsh areas along the southwest coast of Hudson Bay until October, when the first snow falls, then leave for the south. During their stay, they sometimes fly inland to feed, but don't leave the area until they build up body strength.
Severn River	Spring	May 20th	June 15th	Feeding, nesting	Most snow geese leave Severn River area by mid-June, flying out to the bay; in recent years, some have started staying to nest—the number depending on weather conditions.
	Fall	Middle of August	End of September, October	Feeding	In fall, snow geese have been flying west when leaving the Hudson Bay area and, since 1979, have been leaving a little earlier. Flying west from the Fort Severn area puts the flyway directly over the Manitoba Hydro water-catchment areas.
Shamattawa	Fall	First of September	End of October	Passing through	Snow geese migrate through Shamattawa from the beginning of September to the end of October.

Community/Region	Species/Season	Arrive	Leave	Nest, Moult, Feed, or Pass Through	Comments
York Factory/Marsh Point	Spring	April 20	End of April	Passing through	Marsh Point is a staging area that snow and Canada geese use for feeding during their spring and fall migrations. They don't stay long in the area and usually are found farther north from the last part of June until the end of August.
	Fall	Middle of August	September (present) Middle to end of October (past)	Passing through	Changes in water quality and deterioration in the food that geese eat—grass and willows are replacing the marsh vegetation—have been occurring on the west side of Marsh Point at the mouth of the Nelson River. Logs and driftwood coming downstream from Limestone Rapids, the last dam built on the river, are piling up at the river mouth and along the shorelines, reducing the available feeding area for geese at Marsh Point. Where they used to stay until mid- or the end of October, they now stay only about two weeks any time during the month of September.
Arviat	Spring, Summer	When sea ice is melting	Middle to end of August	Nesting, moulting	Snow geese, one of the most populous birds found in the Arviat area in spring, nest there by the thousands. They produce their eggs later than brants.
Roggan River	Past and present			Feeding	Fifty years ago, snow geese were so abundant on the north side of the Roggan River that Fort George (Chisasibi) residents could hear them feeding and moving around. The geese have been affected by environmental impacts and vegetation changes. Today, there are hardly any geese and the vegetation has overgrown.
Eastern James Bay Coast Eastern James Bay	Spring Spring/Fall			Feeding (mountain belt)	The length of time they stop depends on the wind. They don't stop if there are strong southwest winds. They remain at their previous resting/staging area or they pass right through. Arrive between May 20-29th; migrate in the fall during late October.
Lake Harbour	Spring Fall	June Early September	June September	Passing through Passing through	Snow geese are rarely seen in the Lake Harbour area because of the mountains, hills, and rough terrain. With no marsh for feeding they continue flying farther north—especially east of Lake Harbour—onto Baffin Island. Some snow geese pass through in small numbers about 30 kilometres west of Lake Harbour, but they very seldom fly over this area during their nesting period.
Cape Dorset	Spring	First of June to middle of June	Early September	Passing through, nesting	Snow geese fly over Cape Dorset in greater numbers than over Lake Harbour. They travel east of Cape Dorset where the land isn't rough. They lay their eggs in the *Natsilik* area, on the west side of Tessik Lake.
Canada, Brant, and Blue Goose Summary Information					
Moose Factory	Canada Geese: Fall Blue Geese: Fall	September 20th August 10th (present)	End of October (past) September 20th (present)	Feeding	Moose Factory is the last staging area for Canada geese flying south. Since the 1940s, there are fewer Canada geese and they stay for a shorter time because of vegetation changes. Willows, brush, and grass are growing in primary coastal feeding areas; the geese tend to fly inland to feed on berries during the day, then return to the coast in the evening.
Western James Bay: Fort Albany, Attawapiskat	Canada Geese: Spring	End of April (past) First part of June (present)	April to mid-June	Spring migration	From 1948 to 1968, Canada geese arrived at the end of April. Spring behaviour of migrating Canada geese began changing noticeably about 1984, when more Canada geese started coming into the area from the west than from the south. This was particularly so in the spring of 1993, when Canada geese arrived first in communities farther north than western James Bay. Community representatives have heard CB radio reports sighting geese in Fort Severn before they are sighted in Moosonee. They fly into western James Bay from the north in the first part of June. When it is warm enough, they arrive earlier, first in the southwestern area of Hudson Bay, then into western James Bay.

Community/ Region	Species/ Season	Arrive	Leave	Nest, Moult, Feed, or Pass Through	Comments
Attawapiskat River	Canada Geese: Spring, Summer, Fall	End of April	Mid-October	Feeding, migrating	Canada geese began moving into the Attawapiskat River-Swan River area in the summer of 1988 and, by 1992, were gathering in large numbers with their goslings upstream on the main Attawapiskat River in summer. Although there are many geese in the Attawapiskat-Swan River area in the fall, they don't seem to return in the spring, leading community representatives to think they arrive from the northern coastal areas of southwestern Hudson Bay. The only geese migrating into the Attawapiskat area in spring are the nesting geese and greater Canada geese.
Cape Henrietta Maria	Canada Geese: Fall	End of May	Beginning of September	Nesting	Canada geese nest with snow geese in the Cape Henrietta Maria area. The two species eat different plants and Canada geese remain in the same nesting area until their fall migration.
Western James Bay	Canada Geese: Fall	September	Mid-October	Migrating	As with snow geese, more Canada geese have been migrating to the west in the fall rather than taking the coastal route south. For this reason, people now see fewer Canada geese in the western James Bay area than they did in the past.
Peawanuck	Canada Geese: Fall (past)	End of August	Mid-October	Feeding	Fifty years ago, Canada geese left in mid-October and flew straight south. They were the first of the geese to leave.
Severn River	Canada Geese: Spring & Summer	May 20th	Third week of September to first week of October	Nesting (May to mid-June) Moulting (July, August)	Fully grown when they arrive in spring, some Canada geese stay to nest and moult in the Fort Severn area. June weather is a critical factor for nesting; a snow storm, for example, can freeze their eggs.
Shamattawa	Canada Geese: Spring Canada Geese: Fall	Mid-April	Mid-April September & October	Spring migration Fall migration	Canada geese usually arrive about the 15-18th of April, unless it is too cold. In fall, they migrate south from the beginning of September to the end of October.
York Factory/ Marsh Point	Canada Geese: Spring	End of April to Mid-June	Mid-June	Spring migration	Marsh Point is a staging area that snow and Canada geese use for feeding and resting during their spring and fall migrations. They don't stay long in the area and usually are found farther north from the last part of June until the end of August.
	Canada Geese: Fall	September (past)	Mid to end of October (past)	Fall migration, passing through, feeding	Canada geese used to migrate through the area from the middle to the end of October.
		September (present)	September (present)		They now return from the north, flying in from Hudson Bay and swinging west through York Factory any time during September, staying for only about two weeks. Changes in water quality and deterioration in the food that geese eat—grass and willows are replacing the marsh vegetation—have been occurring on the west side of Marsh Point at the mouth of Nelson River. Logs and driftwood coming downstream from Limestone Rapids, the last dam built on the river, are piling up at the river mouth and along the shorelines, reducing the available feeding area for geese at Marsh Point.
Arviat	Brants: Spring & Summer	June, early July	Middle to end of August	Nesting, moulting	Brant geese arrive in the Arviat area with snow geese during spring. Brants nest by the thousands in marshland south of the community towards Churchill. They lay their eggs much earlier than other geese and ducks and leave the area immediately after moulting.
	Canada Geese: Spring	June, early July	June, early July	Passing through	Geese are flying north to nesting/moulting areas.
Rankin Inlet, Chesterfield Inlet	Canada Geese: Summer	End of June	End of August	Nesting, moulting	Many Canada geese nest in the area between Rankin Inlet and Chesterfield Inlet.

Community/ Region	Species/ Season	Arrive	Leave	Nest, Moult, Feed, or Pass Through	Comments
Wager Bay, Repulse Bay, Southampton Island	Canada Geese: Summer	End of June, July	Hard to notice	Moulting	There are few Canada geese in the Repulse Bay area, although numbers were greater during the summers of 1992 and 1993. Many Canada geese moult between Wager Bay and Repulse Bay, and even more moult in the Coral Harbour area of Southampton Island. The brants lay eggs on an offshore island near Wager Bay. Some also nest in coastal bluffs and on islands in lakes.
Wager Bay	Brants	June	End of August, September	Nesting	
Roggan River, Eastern James Bay Coast	Canada Geese: Spring	End of April, May	Immediately	Passing through	The first batch of Canada geese arrives in late April and early May, stopping to feed only once before flying north to nest. This group has declined in numbers since 1988. The second batch—greater Canada geese—arrives in late spring only to moult. These geese are larger in size than Canada geese and fly in great numbers, landing to moult in coastal areas, river mouths, and on islands in the bays. They are first to migrate south and are hunted by coastal Cree during the migration period from the end of August to early September.
	Greater Canada Geese (i.e., Long-necks)	Early–mid-June	Early September; gone by September 10th	Moulting	
Belcher Islands	Canada Geese	Mid-April to end of May	Mid-August	Nesting and moulting	Canada geese have arrived in smaller flocks since 1984, when strong winds began to blow from the north between late April and the end of May. People seldom see Canada geese coming in anymore. They still nest in the islands, but by the time they are found they are already preparing to nest. Some nesting Canada geese start flying again in late July, early August. They immediately get ready to leave the islands and start flying south by the middle of August. Greater Canada geese come only to moult and have been arriving in very large numbers since 1991. They first arrive near the end of May and continue to the first week of July. These geese are not afraid of people and don't try to get away when hunted. The length of time blue geese stop depends on the wind; if there are strong southwest winds, they don't stop.
Belcher Islands	Greater Canada Geese	End of May–June–first week of July	Towards end of September	Moulting	
	Blue Geese: Spring	Mid-May	September	Passing through	
Eastern Hudson Bay	Greater Canada Geese: Spring & Summer	June, first week of July	Towards end of September	Moulting	The greater Canada geese are found moulting all along the eastern Hudson Bay coast up to Ivujivik. They come in large numbers about a month after the nesting geese arrive.
Salluit	Canada Geese: Spring & Summer Greater Canada Geese: Spring & Summer	End of May	August	Feeding, moulting	Both species moult in the Salluit area. The greater Canada geese moult between Salluit and Kangiqsujuaq, which is also a feeding area for Canada geese. Canada geese leave the feeding ground when they are ready to lay their eggs.
Lake Harbour	Canada Geese: Spring	June	Mid-August	Nesting (June), moulting (July, August)	Two migrations of Canada geese arrive in spring. The first migration is adults that stop to nest in the area. They no longer nest in the Soper River heritage area because of increased human activity. Once geese are aware of human activity they move away and find other places to nest. The second migration is younger geese. They arrive in larger numbers and pass through to moult in areas with lots of open space and smooth terrain. They moult very fast and return from the north when the berries ripen. While passing through, they eat large numbers of berries.
	Canada Geese: Fall	August	End of August	Passing through	

Appendix F: Hudson Bay Programme Reports

During the Hudson Bay Programme, eight technical papers on the bioregion were produced. These papers, which provide detailed information beyond that presented in *Voices from the Bay*, are available from the Canadian Arctic Resources Committee, One Nicholas Street, Suite 1100, Ottawa, Ontario, Canada K1N 7B7; telephone: (613) 241-7379.

1. *Human Impacts on the Hudson Bay Region, its Present State and Future Environmental Concerns.* P. G. Sly. Hudson Bay Programme. 1993. 149 pp. ($15.00).
   ISBN: 0-919996-50-7.

This paper presents a comprehensive assessment of the state of scientific knowledge about the Hudson Bay bioregion. Environmental effects of past and current development projects in the region are only now beginning to be understood, and potential impacts arising from proposed projects around the bay are still unclear. Hence there is a critical need for scientific information about the region to guide researchers and policy makers in their decisions regarding past, present, and future developments. *Human Impacts on the Hudson Bay Region, its Present State and Future Environmental Concerns* also sets the scene for more detailed research on those components of the Hudson Bay bioregion that will tell us most about the likely long-term impacts of future developments there. This report has been organized into the following categories: the watershed; settlement and land-use patterns; the bay and its ecosystem; environmental stress and possible causes; identifying and understanding the concern; and cumulative impact evaluation. It will be of use to scientists and non-scientists alike who have an interest in the Hudson Bay bioregion.

2. *Towards the Assessment of Cumulative Impacts in Hudson Bay.* John Sallenave (ed.). Hudson Bay Programme. 1993. 41 pp. ($10.00).
   ISBN: 0-919996-51-5.

This report presents the proceedings of a workshop hosted by the Hudson Bay Programme in May 1993 to determine the areas of research that needed to be addressed to assess the cumulative impacts of past and present developments in the Hudson Bay bioregion. The workshop was also charged with identifying information gaps in scientific knowledge of the Hudson Bay bioregion and determining the best methods of addressing those gaps. The report features presentations on cumulative impact assessment by experts in the field and a summary of the discussion. Topics include an overview of the Hudson Bay Programme; approaches to cumulative impact assessment; the use of traditional ecological knowledge (TEK); the relationship between TEK and science; and assessing natural viability versus human-induced impacts.

3. *Health Effects of Development in the Hudson Bay/James Bay Region.* David Stieb and Katherine Davies. Hudson Bay Programme. 1994. 45 pp. ($15.00).
   ISBN: 0-919996-52-3.

This literature review reveals that, despite recent measurable improvements, the health of native people in the Hudson Bay/James Bay region still is considerably worse than that of other Canadians. Chronic diseases such as obesity, diabetes, and high blood pressure have become more prevalent and injuries, poisonings, and violence are at epidemic levels. The authors suggest that social, economic, and cultural changes in the region's communities, which have profoundly affected native self-sufficiency and, in turn, their identity and well-being, are the major reason for these alarming trends.

4. *Climate Variability, Climatic Change, and Implications for the Future of the Hudson Bay Bioregion.* S. J. Cohen, T. A. Agnew, A. Headley, P. Louie, J. Reycraft, and W. Skinner. Hudson Bay Programme. 1994. 113 pp. ($40.00).
   ISBN: 0-919996-56-6.

Patterns of air temperature, precipitation, ice cover, soil temperature, and stream flow are documented in this comprehensive review of the climate of the Hudson Bay bioregion. The patterns are described for instrumental record in graphs and multi-coloured maps. The authors also examine recent climatic trends and use climate model projections to draw scenarios of greenhouse gas-induced climatic change and their implications for ecosystems around Hudson Bay. They identify a need for increased monitoring of snow cover, stream flow in unregulated rivers, and freshwater ice and propose that an integrated regional assessment of scenarios of climatic changes and water resource development be undertaken.

5. *The Estuaries of Hudson Bay: A Case Study of the Physical and Biological Characteristics of Selected Sites.* F. Schneider-Vieira, R. Baker, and M. Lawrence. Hudson Bay Programme. 1994. 36 pp. ($15.00). ISBN: 0-919996-54-X.

Five sites—the Churchill estuary, the Nelson estuary, La Grande estuary, the Eastmain estuary, and Chesterfield Inlet, which encompass a range of estuarine environments—are described to illustrate general estuarine processes. Four of these sites have been affected by hydroelectric development. The authors examine the food webs in these estuaries and discuss phytoplankton, benthic animal, fish, and beluga populations. They suggest that the physical changes caused by hydroelectric development have not altered the anadromous lake cisco and lake whitefish population.

6. *Native Land Use, Traditional Knowledge and the Subsistence Economy in the Hudson Bay Bioregion.* Helen Fast and Fikret Berkes. Hudson Bay Programme. 1994. 33 pp. ($15.00). ISBN: 0-919996-53-1.

The authors summarize some 15 land-use studies from all major parts of the Hudson Bay bioregion. Aboriginal harvesting of wildlife (hunting, fishing, and trapping) is the dominant land use, and it shapes the relationship between human societies and the environment. The authors provide examples where use of the land is based on traditional ecological knowledge and environmental management systems of the people. The report examines subsistence economies, including their significance in different regions, and development projects that have affected these economies. The authors contend that strengthening the bush economy would improve the quality of life of aboriginal peoples in the bioregion.

7. *Effects of Hydroelectric Projects on Hudson Bay's Marine and Ice Environments.* Simon J. Prinsenberg. Hudson Bay Programme. 1994. 20 pp. ($10.00). ISBN: 0-919996-55-8.

Prinsenberg examines how the hydroelectric development in the Hudson Bay region affects the timing and amplitude of run-off rates and thus alters oceanographic and ice-cover properties of the region. He presents the known oceanographic and ice-cover properties of the bays and suggests possible changes in winter oceanographic and ice-cover conditions as a result of hydroelectric developments. In addition, he refers to models that predict the strength of winter estuarine circulation in James Bay, size of plumes outside rivers affected by hydro projects, trends in vertical nutrient fluxes, and thickness and duration of the bay's ice cover.

8. *Traditional Ecological Knowledge of Environmental Changes in Hudson and James Bays, Parts I & II.* L. Arragutainaq, M. McDonald, Z. Novalinga, T. Saunders, M. Anderson and S. Hill. Hudson Bay Programme. 1995. Part I, 97 pp. and Part II, 64 pp. + appendices ($40.00 each).

This report presents results of the Traditional Ecological Knowledge and Management Systems (TEKMS) study among the Cree and Inuit who live and continue to depend upon living resources in the Hudson Bay bioregion. The study was conducted for purposes of including traditional ecological knowledge in a cumulative impact assessment of environmental changes occurring as a result of human activities in the Hudson Bay bioregion.

The report is organized into two parts. Part I focuses attention on ways Cree and Inuit have observed the Hudson Bay environment to function and change over the past 50 years. Part II describes the study methods and reviews the information database developed during the study. It also presents Cree and Inuit knowledge on certain components of the ecosystem to demonstrate the technical and detailed manner in which they know and understand their environment. Several GIS-generated maps are included in Part II to support information discussed in Part I.